A COUNTRYSIDE FOR ALL

Michael Sissons was until recently Chairman of the Peters Fraser & Dunlop Group and was a founder of the Countryside Movement.

A COUNTRYSIDE FOR ALL

The Future of Rural Britain

EDITED BY
Michael Sissons

VINTAGE

Published by Vintage 2001

2 4 6 8 10 9 7 5 3 1

First published in Great Britain by
Vintage

Vintage
Random House, 20 Vauxhall Bridge Road,
London SW1V 2SA

Random House Australia (Pty) Limited
20 Alfred Street, Milsons Point, Sydney,
New South Wales 2061, Australia

Random House New Zealand Limited
18 Poland Road, Glenfield,
Auckland 10, New Zealand

Random House (Pty) Limited
Endulini, 5A Jubilee Road, Parktown 2193, South Africa

The Random House Group Limited Reg. No. 954009
www.randomhouse.co.uk

A CIP catalogue record for this book
is available from the British Library

ISBN 0099 42889 X

Papers used by Random House are natural, recyclable products made from
wood grown in sustainable forests. The manufacturing processes conform to
the environmental regulations of the country of origin

Printed and bound in Great Britain by
Bookmarque Ltd, Croydon, Surrey

To my dear grandchildren Emily, Francesca and Jack Elvis, in the hope that there will be a green and pleasant land for them to love and enjoy as there has been for me.

Michael Sissons

CONTENTS

PREFACE AND ACKNOWLEDGEMENTS

Michael Sissons

THE COUNTRYSIDE GROUP is an independent think-tank which was formed in 1998 with the objectives of clarifying rural issues and formulating rural policies. A group of us had been centrally involved in the formation of the Countryside Movement and were thus committed to the widest possible framework for the discussion of rural and environmental problems. The format on which we settled was to set up a regular series of monthly meetings over an eighteen-month period, with topics carefully chosen to compose in due course a full mosaic of countryside issues. At each of these meetings a guest speaker with a particular expertise was invited to provide the framework for a discussion of a specific matter to take place. As our perceptions of the central issues developed, we invited others to contribute to the range of subjects covered here. This book is the result.

It does not claim to be exhaustive. The political debate over rural transport, shops and schools is barely touched on. Nor is the price of fuel in rural areas, which remains an explosive issue. Rather we have tried to define a logical framework within which to prescribe a future for the countryside. In the shadow of the foot-and-mouth epidemic, rural Britain needs more than ever political leadership committed to long-term goals.

The core members of the Countryside Group were Richard Benyon, Willie Peel, Roger Scruton and Nick Herbert. Alan

Kilkenny has also given generously of his time. I would particularly like to thank Sophie Scruton, the Group's secretary, who organised the meetings and took the minutes which, in some cases, have formed the basis of the essays reproduced here. Thanks are also due to Sir Christopher Lewinton, who made a generous contribution of seed-corn money, and to the hundreds of country people whom I've met during the past decade through my involvement in rural campaigning. My roots, on both sides of my family, are deep in rural Yorkshire. I have worked all my life in the media. The past decade has given me the chance to retrace my rural steps and realise how much I still had to learn about the British landscape and its people, who deserve well of their country.

In respect of publication, my contributors and I owe a very deep debt of gratitude to Caroline Michel, Publisher of Vintage, and to her colleagues at Random House. She rode over the hill like the 7th Cavalry, and turned this book round from disk to publication in under six weeks. My warm thanks also to my assistant James Gill, whose work in preparing this text went beyond the call of duty.

My love of hunting is known in rural circles. But you will not find in these pages a discussion of the case for field sports, the arguments for and against which have been very fully deployed by the Burns Inquiry into Hunting with Dogs. I do not believe that any fair-minded person coming afresh to this vexed issue will find in its pages an argument for banning hunting by legislation.

Michael Sissons
Broadleaze Farm
March 2001

2

FOREWORD

Robert Skidelsky

THE COUNTRYSIDE HAS been a 'problem' ever since the
Industrial Revolution of the late eighteenth century shifted the
balance of national life from agriculture to manufacturing and
from country to town, and the transport and refrigeration
revolution of the late nineteenth century shifted comparative
advantage from high-cost European producers to the prairie
farming of the New World. The latter, in particular, threatened
most forms of European farming with extinction. These
developments produced a strong reaction against free trade,
which took its principled stand on the need for a 'balanced'
economy as a vital ingredient of social and political health, and
agriculture as a strategic national resource in a warlike world.
Continental Europe restored agricultural protection from the
1870s onwards. Britain, with overseas supplies of cheap food
secured by the Royal Navy and its imperial connections,
continued with free trade in food. British farming survived by
switching from arable to pastoral and then specialising in 'cash
crops' – fruit, vegetables, dairy products – which could be
readily marketed locally. But by the turn of the century less than
10% of the workforce worked on the land and 'long before
1939 it had become second nature to the farmers to complain
that the government was not doing enough for them'.[1]

[1] Sayers, R.S., *A History of Economic Change in England
1880–1939*, OUP (1967), p. 107

Among the opponents of free trade were those who attached particular virtue to the activities of the soil. But the deeper *motif* of the protectionist movement was the belief that a society – by which the protectionists meant a national state – was spiritually deformed if it did not offer its citizens the chance to develop and display the full range of their talents and interests. Keynes eloquently expressed this position when he wrote in 1933: 'To say that a country cannot afford agriculture is to delude oneself about the meaning of the word "afford". A country which cannot afford art or agriculture, invention or tradition, is a country in which one cannot afford to live'.[2]

In practice, the doctrine of free trade in food was held in check by two world wars and the Great Depression of the 1930s. Agriculture became a 'strategic' industry: home-grown food not only guarded against wartime blockade but protected the peacetime balance of payments. For most of the twentieth and twenty-first centuries agriculture has been protected in all developed countries by a mixture of subsidies, price-fixing, tariffs and import quotas: the Common Agricultural Policy (CAP) of the European Union is the main contemporary example of the second. It is easy to show that, under these arrangements, the welfare of consumers has suffered: they have had to pay more for their food. By the same token, non-EU producers have been damaged.

Today these traditional arguments for supporting farming have wilted. In particular, the CAP has produced large surpluses ('mountains') of produce which are expensive to stockpile and difficult to sell off. The global movement towards free trade in food, spearheaded by the World Trade Organisation, coincides with the growing dominance in retailing of the supermarket chains, which have destroyed most of the remaining local advantages enjoyed by the British farmer. The consumerist perspective is once more dominant.

[2] Keynes, J.M., 'Pros and Cons of Tariffs', *Listener*, 30 November 1932. Reprinted in the *Collected Writings of J.M. Keynes*, pub. by Macmillan for the Royal Economic Society, vol. xxi, pp. 209–210

Moreover, it is an overwhelmingly urban perspective – one with little experience or understanding of country life; and, among powerful minorities, showing considerable hostility to its values. Many of those who live and work in the country-side, and care about its future, feel themselves to be an endangered species, alienated from the majority and faced by indifferent or hostile governments.

The current 'crisis of the countryside', identified by contributors to this volume, consists of four threats: the threat to the landscape from urban and industrial 'development'; the threat to natural habitats from pesticides and over-exploitation; the threat to farming from a mixture of free trade, supermarkets and over-regulation; and the threat to rural pursuits and values from class war and/or humanitarian legislation. Despite differences in emphases, and less than ideal clarity about policy – for countryside politics is as riven as urban politics – there is a great deal of coherence here in the underlying analysis. The following areas of broad agreement are striking and need to be emphasised:

1. The authors reject the 'national park' view of the country-side, with its corollary that national policy should be directed to preserving designated areas of great natural beauty for the recreation and solace of city dwellers and other tourists, while being indifferent to whether the rest of the countryside becomes a giant suburb. They believe that the British countryside is a mainly person-made habitat, whose maintenance depends on the existence and flourishing of a rural economy.

2. The authors agree that the bedrock of the rural economy is farming. They also agree, though, that the traditional subsidy policy, whether by the earlier deficiency payments to farmers or the later price-support schemes of the CAP, has had its day. Farmers should see themselves, and be supported, as custodians of the countryside. Subsidies should go not to food production as such, but to land-scape management and to those micro-services which encourage a local food economy (local abattoirs; a village

shop, post office, and school; good public transport services).

3. Traditional subsidy policies – supported by organisations like the National Farmers' Union (NFU) – are criticised for creating rural dependency, stifling entrepreneurship and, in the long run, antagonising consumers, since it has ceased to be clear for what extra services farmers are being paid.

4. It seems to be generally agreed that sections of British agriculture at least could be competitive without protection, through aggressive marketing, reduction in red tape, and the correct pricing of competitor developments which make a local food economy unviable – for example, Roger Scruton argues that supermarkets receive implicit subsidies in the form of 'low peripheral rates, road networks geared to their requirements and planning permissions . . . free from aesthetic constraints'.

5. The authors agree that the fate of town and countryside are intertwined. For example, the suburbanisation of the countryside has been powerfully driven by the decay of cities. They argue that the survival of the countryside which they want depends on a new 'social contract' between town and country, based on the idea of rural custodianship. This requires compromise in such contentious areas as field sports and the right to roam. Farmers will only remain custodians of the countryside if it is both profitable and agreeable to them to live and work there. But, as Roger Scruton writes, they must be induced 'to accept whatever incursions might be necessary if their privileges are to be maintained'.

Agreement on policies to resolve the rural crisis is harder to find. Should the aim be to encourage higher urban densities to relieve pressure on greenfield sites, or should some overflow development be allowed in order to protect the 'deep' countryside from urban sprawl? The biggest debate is on the respective roles of planning and economic instruments in rescuing rural life. Should one put an 'absolute stop on rural land development', as Simon Jenkins wants? Should one rely on tax incentives and disincentives to achieve the same goal? Or should one (sensibly) recognise, with Mark Pennington, that planning, regulation and market incentives all have a part to play in reversing urban and rural decay?

Where, then, does an outsider to this debate discover solid economic ground for pro-countryside policies? One line of argument is that the maintenance of the countryside confers benefits to visitors ('tourists') who cannot readily be charged for it. Farmers and country dwellers can be likened to artists. They create beautiful landscapes which can be enjoyed by all, but which cannot be bought by anyone. They should therefore be paid for their services. This is a standard argument for state subsidy. Some such argument plainly lies behind the shift in the CAP to paying farmers to 'manage' land rather than produce food. But 'land management' is a vaguer idea than food production, and under bureaucratic direction, can produce such monstrosities as endless spruce planting.

The countryside can also be regarded as a 'merit good' – a good which expresses community values rather than personal preferences, and which may therefore require budgetary support. We may accept that the existence of the countryside is good, even though we rarely or never use it. Why? Because we are inescapably products of a culture in which country life is highly prized, and this influences our attitude towards it, if not necessarily our tastes.

There is a third argument. Specialisation may increase economic welfare, but, as both Adam Smith and Karl Marx pointed out, it diminishes human significance. To become a cog in a productive machine was the price to be paid for economic progress. However, perhaps this process of turning human beings into specialised factors of production has reached the point of diminishing returns. There is ample evidence, in developed countries at least, that economic growth yields negligible amounts of extra happiness.[3] A

[3] See Andrew Oswald, 'Happiness and Economic Performance', Warwick University Economics Department Research Paper, no. 478, 1997.

plausible inference from this finding is that people still get extra utility from having more material goods and services, but that this is almost exactly balanced by a loss of utility in other areas of life; a loss which is not captured by conventional indices of progress like per capita GDP growth. So the ideal of a 'balanced' economy, which attends to the satisfaction afforded by activities and ways of life rather than only to their cost, comes into its own again.

These theoretical considerations put the case for the countryside on firmer foundations than those of nostalgia or romanticism. But they rest in the last analysis on a value judgement in favour of preserving rural life. They cannot be reduced to Bentham's 'felicific calculus'.

Also they cannot tell us exactly what to do. The case for subsidy has to be balanced against the often burdensome regulation which subsidy brings – and constant government assault on the rural way of life at the behest of the largely urban taxpayer. So there is a case for trusting the ingenuity and resourcefulness of the rural population, which now includes large numbers of 'reverse commuters', to find their own ways of surviving and flourishing.

One clear message which emerges from the discussion is that the health of town and country is interdependent. Housing, businesses and people are forced out on to greenfield sites by high urban prices, while large areas of big cities are derelict, congested and crime-ridden. Urban renewal, which makes possible higher densities, a safer environment and more efficient transport, is thus one of the keys to rural survival. How to achieve this – by what mixture of better planning and policing, deregulation and use of the price mechanism – is a matter of hard policy, and hard political choices.

My second thought is that one of the best ways to preserve 'communities in the countryside' is to preserve, and all too often re-establish, village schools. The merger mania of the 1960s and 1970s, which spread from business to education and liquidated hundreds of village primaries in the belief that big is inevitably better, is now seen to have been as misguided in the one sphere as in the other. But I personally would want to leave the re-creation of village schools to local and private initiative. To renew and support a school, possibly embedded in a small community centre, would be a fine act of mingled altruism and self-interest for a local community, especially one enriched by an influx of wealthy commuters.

Supporters of the countryside form a motley army. It could scarcely be otherwise with so many criss-crossing interests and aims. What this timely book does is to outline the main problems facing the countryside, and start to bring together a coherent set of policies for reversing what Michael Sissons calls 'the atrophy of the rural economy and way of life'.

A Managed Landscape

A CONSERVATIVE VIEW OF THE COUNTRYSIDE

Roger Scruton

THE COUNTRYSIDE HAS become an icon of national loyalty, a symbol of what is most precious to us, and at the same time an example of the fragility of our attachments. The threat to the landscape from building, from roads, from industry and agribusiness, is apparent to almost everyone. But the countryside is more than just landscape: it is people, agriculture and wildlife, bound together in a common destiny. The rural economy is now under increasing pressure from global forces that it cannot control. The rural way of life is threatened by legislative encroachment and suburbanisation. And wildlife is being driven to extinction by pesticides, fertilisers, drainage and the over-exploitation of natural resources. Hence all political parties have become aware of the need for a rural policy. The Conservative Party, which has complacently relied upon the rural vote, must now address the concerns of a rural population increasingly troubled by the pressures bearing in upon it from outside.

A PRINCIPLED POLICY FOR THE COUNTRYSIDE
1.   *The Problem of Reverse Commuting*
The first principle that any conservative ought to endorse, is that the countryside owes its identity, its beauty and its character to the people who live and work in it. No policy of

conservation makes sense which does not count people among the things that must be conserved.

The flight from the land to the cities, lamented by William Cobbett, has now been reversed. But the land does not benefit, since those now moving into the countryside commute to their workplace in the towns, and make no economic and little social contribution to the local life. They shop in urban supermarkets, make no use of public transport, and are seldom seen in church or pub. Meanwhile, those who work on the land cannot afford to live there, since the commuters have driven the price of housing beyond their means. Hence there is now a reverse commuting, with farmers and farm labourers living in cheap lodgings in the towns and driving out to their place of work. This means that the old local economy, in which those who lived on the land also worked there, and vice versa, has been severely damaged, and with it the system of mutual support and commitment to the locality that was so vital in making the countryside what it is. Local shops and pubs expire, young people leave for the towns, and old people become increasingly isolated, deprived of services, transport and the means of survival.

In the light of this, there is clear need for a wholly new and radical conservative policy, designed to protect the social as well as the natural ecology of the countryside, and to encourage the restoration of local services, local economies, and affordable housing for those with a title to the landscape – namely, those who shoulder the burden of maintaining it.

2. *People are Trustees of the Land*

The second principle of conservative policy is that of trusteeship. The environment can no longer be relied upon to reproduce itself and the wildlife that inhabits it. People are guardians and trustees of the land, and they must be encouraged to look after it. This means that any subsidies offered to those who sustain the rural economy ought to be attached first and foremost to residence, and to activities which help the land to renew itself. Current policies favour the absentee exploiter over the resident farmer and environmentally damaging monoculture over the small-scale mixed farming which created and maintained our traditional landscape.

3. *A Family Inheritance to Cherish and Bequeath*
The third principle is that of inheritance. The beauty of the British countryside is almost entirely due to the fact that it has been owned by families across generations – whether in the form of landed estates or family farms. Those who inherit property and pass it on have a motive to look after it that is quite different from the motive of the temporary resident. Ill-considered taxes have penalised inheritance, broken up the landed estates, and now threaten the family farm. A coherent conservative policy must first try to reverse this process, so as to facilitate the long-term interest in the land across generations. Currently the National Trust and the Forestry Commission – both beneficiaries of inheritance tax – are the largest absentee landlords in the country.

4. *Encourage the Small and Local*
a. Family farms vs. agribusiness
The family farm is the backbone of the rural economy, and the most important generator of the distinctive British land-scapes. Fiscal policy must be designed in order to make the family farm once again viable. This means abolishing the regulations that make it unprofitable, and encouraging the local food economy, local slaughterhouses and farmers' markets. Many of these regulations proceed from the EU; others are either imposed by Ministry of Agriculture, Fisheries and Food or derived from the EU by over-rigorous interpretation of its edicts. Some are the result of pressure from the food safety lobby, and from the organised hypochondriacs who pretend to speak for the nation in the matter of what we eat. Whatever the origin, however, it is now clear that regulations are killing off small farms, seriously compromising the old forms of husbandry and producing few proven benefits in either human or animal welfare. The principal beneficiaries are agribusiness and the

large-scale food distributors, who can afford to comply with regulations that drive their small competitors out of business. A coherent conservative policy must tackle the issue of regulation head-on, and set about reviving the local food economy that has made rural life sustainable. It must also be prepared to protect our small producers from unfair or subsidised competition. Countries which do not conform to our welfare standards in the production of pork or chicken meat, for example, must be subjected to import restrictions.

b. Small-scale industry vs. industrial estates
If the rural economy is to be revitalised, a part must also be played by small-scale local industry, and by the injection of new capital from the cities. Some hard thinking needs to be done about the ways and means to integrate small-scale industry into the landscape, while avoiding the destructive proliferation of 'industrial estates' which have no real social or economic relation to the life surrounding them.

c. High street shops vs. out-of-town supermarkets
The threats posed to market towns and the food economy by the supermarket chains must be acknowledged and countered. This means a radical revision in planning laws, and the adoption of policies designed to force the out-of-town superstore to internalise its costs. As things stand, the supermarket chains are beneficiaries of massive subsidies, in the form of low peripheral rates, road networks geared to their requirements, and planning permissions for large-scale greenfield developments free from aesthetic constraints. In a genuine market economy, the high street shop would be able to compete with them. But because the supermarkets can externalise so many of their costs, they are able to destroy any local competition.

5. *Dealing with Sources of Rural–Urban Antagonism*
The potential sources of antagonism between rural and urban people must be identified and if possible neutralised. Two areas are particularly important: field sports and the right to

roam. A process of discussion, negotiation and compromise should begin, with a view to making legislation unnecessary and inducing rural people to accept whatever incursions might be necessary if their privileges are to be maintained. The confrontational approach adopted so far has been counter-productive.

THE REAL ISSUE: DECAYING CITY LIFE

There can be no adequate response to the threat of over-development in the countryside that does not address the real issue, which is the decay of cities and the loss of amenity in urban life. Many of our inner-city areas are now unviable. Schools are dreadful, drugs and promiscuity threaten the young, and crime levels are soaring. The absurd schemes of post-war planners, which resulted in the demolition of good housing in which communities had flourished, and the erection of unliveable towers in which communities expired, are partly responsible for this. But they are not the only cause. Social policy must address the whole question of what makes cities liveable. It must encourage the emergence in inner-city areas of genuine self-policing communities, with effective codes of conduct, good schools, motivated young people and an ethos of self-respect. This cannot be done without consultation with local people, and a willingness to respond to their needs and fears.

There is no way of reviving our inner cities without radical changes in planning: densities must be increased, and streets must be made agreeable. The destructive modernist archetypes must be rejected, and new models devised to replace them – models in which residential housing, business premises, shops, recreational facilities, parks and public buildings all interpenetrate, without clashes of scale or style. The efforts of Leon Krier at Poundbury provide a model for good city planning.

PROTECTION FOR THE COUNTRYSIDE
Revision of the Planning Laws

A revision of the planning laws is also called for, and the first step must be the call for a right of appeal against consent – a right which does not currently exist – together with a moratorium on the number of applications that can be made in a given time. Road-building has become an object of intense controversy in recent years, for the very good reason that roads accelerate the pace of human life, damage wildlife and the environment, and encourage development in the countryside, as well as spoiling the landscape. A far more considered approach is needed, both to the building and the maintenance of roads, and to the kind of building that should occur along their edges.

Holding the Land in Trust

A policy for wildlife must recognise the vital part played by hedgerows, coverts and wetlands. Farmers should be compensated for the expense of maintaining habitats, and penalised where necessary for destroying them.

The interest urban people take in habitats, in archaeological sites and other rural resources, should be encouraged without the Government first permitting unlimited access to the land which will undermine ownership and trusteeship.

The Labour Party tells us that the countryside is a national asset, to be managed for the benefit of the people. But the countryside is a national asset only in the sense that Shakespeare is a national asset. The landscape owes its beauty and its fertility to the fact that it is privately owned. The aim of policy should be to make private ownership into an effective form of trusteeship, so that all of us can benefit from property that only some of us control.

A FUTURE FOR GREEN FIELDS

Simon Jenkins

'"WHAT I LIKE about English rural districts", Psmith remarked on an excursion to Market Blandings, "is that when the authorities have finished building a place they stop. Somewhere about the reign of Henry VIII, the master mason gave the final house a pat with his trowel and said, 'Well boys, that's Market Blandings'. And they went away and left it. It is most soothing."'

Not any more. P.G. Wodehouse would be aghast at modern Market Blandings. Only the church is the same. The rectory is a solicitor's office and the Old Hall is home to the district council. The high street is lined with cut-price stores and charity shops. The pub is a hamburger joint and the market square is the nocturnal haunt of drunks and drug addicts. The place has been killed by Blandings business park, the Tesco on the bypass and the three out-of-town Barratt estates. This is the Shropshire of the future.

Most English people know their country parochially. They know their neighbourhood. They know the corridor that connects it to the nearest town, to the motorway and to London. For most, the concept of a holiday nowadays means overseas. Ask them about their home county and they will confess that it is not what it was. It has been defiled by unsightly farm buildings, out-of-town shops and leisure centres, by motorways, bypasses and housing estates which 'somehow got past the planners'. They will assume such eyesores are local to them. Somewhere beyond must still be Blandings.

They are wrong. Since I first travelled the English countryside twenty-five years ago, eyesores have become the norm: inexcusable caravan sites along the Dorset coast and Yorkshire Dales; new towns springing up at every motorway junction; ancient towns sprawling across their local countrysides. The development of King's Lynn in the 1960s, for instance, brought new businesses in – but at a price. A generation later its mayor, Paul Richards, spoke of its 'intimate and historic street pattern', now lost, its country-town atmosphere snuffed out.

The ideal vision of an English village has a rising visual tempo, from fields, to trees, to cottage roofs and chimneys, all fixed in place by a single, soaring steeple. This graduation has all but gone. Some trees and cottages may survive, but in a visually homogenised landscape of estate housing. Unrestricted development has not been designed to protect the village economy or to contribute to its visual coherence. No thought is given to the appearance of a garish service station, or overhead cables, or road signs. The old village and its church are a mere backdrop for traffic and housing. Cruikshank's *March of Bricks and Mortar* has left London far behind and is rampaging across the countryside. 'The finest crop that a field can grow/Is a hundred houses, all in a row.'

TWO CATASTROPHIC INNOVATIONS

The two most catastrophic innovations of the past twenty years were the end of the 'presumption against development' of agricultural land and the introduction, by the late Lord Ridley in the mid-1980s, of a presumption in favour of out-of-town supermarkets. The latter have had truly enormous impact, both on the countryside itself and on adjacent towns throughout Britain. Now people are beginning to count the cost: each out-of-town superstore cut the market share of in-town food shops by up to 50% and meant an average loss of 276 full-time jobs in the town's streets.

Outside the National Parks there is near-anarchy.

Developers can defy green belts – witness the new town outside Stevenage. They can impose 'planning creep', evolving farm buildings and caravan sites into complete new settlements. They can fill in the fields between towns and motorways. They can use the appeal system to overrule local councils, by threatening costly public inquiries and pleading 'housing need' or 'shopping jobs' to obtain development.

We are now witnessing what planners term the 'donutting' of England. By encouraging such services as supermarkets, leisure centres and business parks on the outskirts of towns, planners are turning suburbs inside out. This means that every journey to work, school or shop requires a car. Roads congest and the cost of public services rises. Meanwhile, town centres degenerate and are impoverished. Such a pattern has been repeated where 'free-market' planning, of the sort espoused by the Tories and continued by the present Government, has guided development in North America, India, Africa or any heavily populated landscape.

In England, enthusiasts need look no further than the outskirts of Exeter, Ely or Derby. They can gaze down on the Gloucester/Cheltenham conurbation from Cleeve Hill in the Cotswolds. The impact of donutting is most fierce in such cities as Bristol, Portsmouth, Leicester or Nottingham, where new out-of-town activities have been encouraged to replace dying inner-city ones. It is repeated in smaller urban centres and even old market towns. You may see it in Worcester or Northampton or the mill towns of Yorkshire and Lancashire. Sparkling out-of-town malls and glittering rural leisure strips may look good on a council brochure; the price lies in the commercial scorched earth left behind. Rural sprawl is threatening the core of every town in England. Killing the countryside also kills the town – it is madness.

REVIVE THE URBAN, SAVE THE RURAL

The argument I meet in every pub and hotel in the land is that this evolution is inevitable. We are powerless before the forces of suburbanisation. Yet there is no 'planning necessity' for a single hectare of green Britain to be consumed for building.

Planning is what the nation decides. Although the much-quoted projected figure of 4.4 million new households required over twenty-five years (1991–2016) is now 3.8 million (for the dates 1996–2021), it is still a massive number. Those new households are not a 'land requirement', any more than similar predictions for cars 'require' more road space. There is no planning reason why the existing stock of land and houses, coupled with the price mechanism, cannot absorb the pressure. Such an approach is government policy on roads. Why not on housing?

In every decade since the Second World War an area of countryside the size of Greater London has been lost. Now every year new buildings swallow up a stretch of country land as large as Bristol (100 sq km). Yet, according to the CPRE, six times that amount of land is lying unused in towns and cities; British Gas puts the figure at 2000 sq km. When 800,000 houses lie empty in cities and millions of public-sector properties are under-occupied, ministers insult public intelligence by claiming that building on green-belt land is essential. The 3.8 million new homes may be what private house-builders want – it is highly profitable to build afresh in green fields – but sensible planning reuses urban land and builds to higher densities where existing services are in place and traffic costs minimised. This may increase property prices. Protecting the environment has a cost. But greenfield development is not a 'necessity'.

Nor is it a matter of equity. Britain is one of Europe's most densely populated countries, yet it has the least densely populated towns and cities. The reason for this is historical. Before the twentieth century, British cities were not constrained by defensive fortifications. They could and did spread. Extensive ribbon development was a British innovation, as was the modern commuter suburb. Yet today, the European nation with the least open countryside per head (outside the Low Countries) is also the one with the weakest will to preserve it. Unless Britain can use planning to revive 'the culture of the town', the breakneck suburbanisation of the country will continue.

Open countryside, too, is under pressure – for wind farms. There are now fifty-seven of these, their turbines 100 m tall. They generate a total of 140 MW; an average gas-fired power station more than doubles that, with 300 MW – which the Sizewell nuclear reactor quadruples. But 'clean green' energy inevitably has its supporters.

A COUNTRYSIDE TO CHERISH

I believe that the countryside must be treated as more than a fleeting pleasure for those lucky enough to grab a patch before the next estate arrives. Countryside scored highest in a recent MORI survey of what the British most like about Britain, above even the Royal Family and the English character. It can still be a place of beauty and a pleasure to visit, quite apart from its ecological importance. As a tourist resource, the countryside saves foreign exchange and reduces pressure on travel. It is a real national asset.

This countryside has long been in the guardianship of farming. Despite the spread of National Parks and holdings of the National Trust, there is no alternative to the farmer as custodian. Many people are deeply sceptical of modern farm practices. Many are fed up with Farmer Greed and Farmer Whinge. But all the scepticism in the world will not find another custodian. Farmers must be kept on the land and the land must be kept, in some sense, viable for farmers. This means accelerating the so-far tentative policy shift away from market intervention towards landscape management. Yet there is no point in doing this if weak planning offers farmers a constant incentive to steal land from the country and give it to the town. One thing is certain: free-market economics will never give it back again. In the whole of history only war and pestilence have ever done that. I prefer to use planning.

I would put an absolute stop on rural land development. I would prosecute local councils for corruption, or for 'sale of development rights' with planning gain. I would insist that all disused government land that was former countryside be returned to that state. The worst eyesores in England are army and air force bases. John Prescott and his ministers should stop fighting on the side of the house-building lobby in the courts, as they are against the local council in Sussex. A ban on greenfield building would redirect the property market to renewing inner towns and cities. It would encourage single-person households to recolonise urban neighbourhoods and revive the urban economy. Planning cannot usurp the market, but it can set the framework in which the market operates.

When I was last in France, my English hosts were up in arms over a proposal to run a TGV train through their valley. It would, they rightly said, ruin one of the loveliest corners of France. They were raising a petition. I asked when they had last petitioned against the desecration of the English countryside. Had they protested against the Cornish wind turbines or a Peak District housing estate? What about the desecration of Gloucestershire or the motorised hell that is Hertfordshire?

They knew nothing of it. England was their dormitory and workplace, no longer the country. Until England's middle classes awaken to the spoliation of England's landscape, there is only one outcome. England will become one large suburb, and for country we shall all go to France.

This essay is based on an article originally published in Country Life *in 1999*

DENATIONALISING THE LAND

Matt Ridley

THE DEFECTS OF nationalisation are now well known. Not even socialists still recommend it for industry. By removing competition and replacing it with bureaucratic control, the nationalisation of an industry gradually strangles it with a lack of innovation, a neglect of investment and a culture of rent-seeking by special interests. This was the fate of land ownership in China, the Soviet Union and most of Eastern Europe following the abolition of private property. It was also the fate of numerous industries in Britain during the 1970s.

We will surely learn enough from history not to make that mistake again. Yet in one area of national life we are already making that mistake again, and it is being done to loud acclaim from all parts of the political spectrum: the ownership of the countryside is being gradually nationalised. It has proceeded with virtually no interruption under Labour and Conservative governments alike.

It is not, of course, called land nationalisation, but usually goes under the name of environmental policy, though it began more in the name of increasing the productivity of agriculture and forestry. Yet the effect is to remove one by one the property rights of landowners large and small and to vest them instead in agencies of the state. There is no dispute that this is happening. There are only a few people, myself among them, who think it is a bad thing. And there are fewer still who recognise the strong historical parallels with what happened in communist countries during the twentieth century.

TAKING OVER THE LAND
The Forestry Commission

It began, like other nationalisations, with direct acquisition of land. In 1919, in response to a shortage of timber during the First World War, the government set up the Forestry Commission with the remit to acquire land with government money, plant it with trees and harvest those trees for the Treasury. This the Forestry Commission proceeded to do with gusto, gradually becoming one of the greatest landowners in the country. It now owns more than 800,000 hectares; in Scotland it owns more than 6% of the entire country.

The Forestry Commission, as befits a nationalised industry, has lost money for eighty years – it typically loses about £50m a year. The original purpose of the Commission was mercantilist: to replace imports. But given Britain's cool summers and high winds, we cannot compete with continental climates at tree-growing. It makes no more sense to subsidise home-grown timber production than home-grown banana production. The whole exercise has been an economic disaster.

State forestry has also been an environmental disaster, replacing native moorland with plantations of exotic Sitka spruce in even-age, densely spaced forests that not only mar landscapes and alter the ecology but offer little employment. Not content with owning its own estate, the Forestry Commission acquired the rights to regulate the trees on private land as well. It did this by subsidising, at first through the tax system, the planting of trees by private landowners. It has now acquired general power over all planting and felling in the countryside. No landowner may fell a wood or replant it without a licence from part of the Commission, which must be sought in sextuplicate and takes a month or more to process. The bureaucracy reserves the right not just to refuse such applications but to micro-manage them – insisting on the planting of certain species of tree, for instance.

The Ministry of Agriculture

Some other arms of government followed the Forestry Commission's example of acquiring land for themselves – county councils were frequent buyers of farms in the 1930s, for instance, and the Ministry of Defence is a big landowner. But bureaucrats soon realised that the direct acquisition of land by the state was unnecessarily expensive, and that the subsidise-and-regulate route offered more possibilities for empire-building. The Ministry of Agriculture, having administered various forms of subsidy since the 1940s, suddenly saw an opportunity in 1992, as a result of the MacSharry reforms to the CAP, to rival the Forestry Commission's grip on its clients. Subsidies were switched from products to land, so MAFF asked farmers to file detailed maps of how every hectare of arable land had been planted every year. As expected, this 'IACS' system gradually became more officious. Any mistake in form-filling by the farmer is punished with a heavy fine, while frequent mistakes by MAFF bureaucrats in processing the forms go unpunished – even if they almost lead to a fine for the farmer, as has happened.

Meanwhile, sheep subsidies led to overgrazing, which was solved, once more, by regulation: sheep-counting is now a national duty. The BSE crisis then gave the MAFF bureaucrats an excuse to issue passports for every cow born in the country, even one that is destined to die within a few days. Again, drastic punishment awaits a farmer who fails to fill in the paperwork correctly.

In farming as in forestry, it was the subsidies that led the landowners into the trap of nationalisation. The bureaucrats' excuse – reasonable enough – was that all the extra regulation was necessary to prevent cheating. But it had the happy side effect of fulfilling Parkinson's Law, that an official is in the business of acquiring extra responsibilities with which to justify extra budget requests and extra subordinates.

POWER TO THE PLANNERS

Meanwhile, the planning laws had begun their long, slow growth. Planning was at first a matter of designating where development could not occur: hence the green belts around cities and the first National Parks. But by the 1990s, it had changed to specifying where development *could* occur. Structure Plans and Regional Planning Guidances became ever more prescriptive, designating some areas for industry, some for housing and some for open space. The lobbying to influence these plans fertilised a whole new industry of planning consultants who were richly rewarded for reports that were weighed rather than read. The result was that development quickly became the preserve of big firms who were able to lobby councils and afford consultants. The individual lost any purchase on the system, which blighted the countryside with large, monotonous developments. Restrictive planning made development highly profitable, which perversely encouraged landowners and developers to pursue it even more vigorously. With 40% of the price of a new house being the land it stood upon, the cost of restriction was borne by the housebuyer and harvested by the landowner.

Development was not just nationalised. It was also centralised. Councils themselves gradually lost their power to decide planning applications, either through the publication of ever-more detailed planning guidances (which made no allowance for local differences) or through the 'calling in' by the Secretary of State for the Environment of controversial applications.

Moreover, in a typical illustration of public choice theory, special interests have gradually captured the planning process for themselves by supplying their expertise to planning authorities. All historic buildings (and an increasing number of ones of dubious value) are 'listed' – which gives English Heritage the power to decide exactly what may be done to them, indeed to *order* that things be done to them. And many of the listings are effectively 'owned' by non-governmental organisations. For instance, English Heritage consults the Georgian Society before approving an alteration to a

Georgian house. Nobody elected the Georgian Society to this position of power over the house owner.

POWER TO THE QUANGOS

An almost exactly analogous process occurred in the natural environment. National Parks and Areas of Outstanding Natural Beauty were invented in the 1940s. In the 1980s they were joined by Sites of Special Scientific Interest, which were initially few and small but have recently grown to include vast areas, such as 'the North Pennines'. Nearly 10% of the entire country is now in an SSSI. Then came Areas of High Landscape Value, Environmentally Sensitive Areas, and Special Conservation Areas. These various acronyms compete for land because they are the expressions of the ambitions of their sponsoring agencies to acquire larger and larger regulatory estates; for with size come budgets and power. Once more, the agencies rely on pressure groups to assist them in their ambitions. English Nature, whose empire is the SSSIs and SCAs (and whose budget quadrupled in fifteen years), barely sneezes without consulting the Royal Society for the Protection of Birds first.

In the battle for closer and closer control of the natural environment, certain wildlife species have proved useful as excuses for demanding restrictive control over private owners. Really rare ones are no good, because they are not present in enough places, so the agencies have increasingly turned to the commoner ones that can be described as 'threatened'. Bats are extremely good in this respect because they are everywhere; so are newts. A well-placed bat or newt can justify an official in interfering with almost anything – from a pylon to a picnic.

The latecomer to the party was the Environment Agency, a child of the privatisation of the water industry. Having lost its estate in the privatisation, the EA has been busy rebuilding it through the regulatory route. It issued more and more prescriptive plans for the management of rivers and the fish, and maximised its budget by quadrupling the price of angling licences (from £14 to £57) even while closing outlying offices and removing most of its staff to the profitable activity of paper-pushing and away from the river bank.

The net effect of all these imperialist quangos is that a landowner can no longer fell a wood, plant a copse, grow a field of corn, graze a sheep, catch a trout, dredge a pond, move a footpath, alter a hedge line or restore a barn without a specific and separate licence for each and every change from the various arms of the bureaucracy. These are all property rights that have effectively been confiscated by the state.

THE LANDOWNERS

To be sure, the landowner still retains certain important property rights. He can usually still shoot a pheasant on his land without permission (in the United States, this is nationalised), she can usually still hunt a fox. They can still exclude trespassers from their land, though they are liable if a trespasser gets injured. Above all, they can sell their land freely to the highest bidder.

But it is surely no accident that these freedoms are exactly the ones that have recently come under attack from the state. Fox hunting is to be banned. Trespassers can no longer be excluded from moor and heath, under the 'right to roam', which may soon be extended to river banks and woodland. And in Scotland even the right to sell to the highest bidder is to be removed from the landowner under land reform legislation being prepared by the Scottish Parliament. It would insist that the landowner offer to sell the land to a consortium of local people (who would in practice be backed by state or lottery grants) at a price to be decided by the state.

It cannot be denied that all this represents creeping nationalisation. But it is not unpopular, even among many landowners who see the good intentions behind the regulatory expansion. Moreover, the process has been quite profitable for most landowners. The subsidies on agriculture, forestry and now environmental projects have been generous. Although much of the subsidy passes straight through the farmer's pocket and into the hands of the farm suppliers, leaving the farmers themselves little better off, they do not generally realise this, and think they are profiting from the subsidies. When the privatisation of the Forestry Commission was mooted under the Major government, a veritable *Who's Who* of dukes and earls rushed to defend state ownership of their benefactor. Landowners, in other words, fatten on the cheese in the mousetrap before it slams shut on them.

But more valuable still have been the planning restrictions, which have granted massive windfalls to those landowners who manage to get land approved for development, and have breathed new life into old barns and steadings, as people rush to live in the few available buildings in the countryside. Britons in the past century proved all too willing to pawn their liberty for cash. Landowners are no exception.

GOOD MOTIVE, BAD END

The motives of the nationalisers are certainly good. They genuinely seek to improve the countryside, according to the definition currently in vogue – productivity, sustainability, biodiversity, whatever. But roads to all sorts of places are paved with good intentions. The objection to land national-isation is not that it would be malicious, but that it would not work. Like all nationalisation, it stifles innovation, removes accountability, centralises decision-making, leads to neglect and will eventually ruin the countryside.

Britain is a patchwork of habitats built by local action, not by national plan. More than any other European country, in the Middle Ages it had strong local property rights vested in individuals, who were free of *dirigiste* control from the centre. As a result the countryside has gardens, hedges, fields, moors, parks and copses because local people had the security of tenure, either as owners or as tenants, which led them to believe that if they invested in their land, they and their children would reap the benefit. Even commons were not free-for-alls: they were simply pieces of joint ownership by a local community. Today the farmer feels that he is working for invisible bureaucrats at MAFF; the landowner dreads the appearance of a rare orchid on her land for behind it come swarms of suited officials to tell her what she cannot do.

Above all, what is lost is variety. However much they pay lip-service to diversity, in practice bureaucrats cannot help imposing centralised uniformity. In the past, land ownership in Britain was probably too concentrated: there were too many earls and not enough smallholders. But earls, unlike ministry officials, did actually live on their land, and did actually contribute to village fêtes or join the parish council. And they were eccentric. One was an agricultural improver; another cared only for the hunting; a third wanted a grand landscape; and so on. That diversity is all now lost.

For a glimpse of the nationalised future, read Ian Mitchell's *Isles of the West* (Edinburgh: Canongate Books, 1999) about the Hebrides, where government conservation bodies have bought up most of the land and are running it with scant respect for local people and local tradition. Decisions are taken in remote Edinburgh offices by faceless absentee landlords who do not even have the redeeming eccentricity of the absentee lairds who went before them.

PROTECTING OUR OWN

There is a feeling abroad that however undesirable some of these trends are, they are inevitable. Nationalisation is the price we have to pay for environmental protection. But this is nonsense of the most pernicious kind. As Mark Pennington argues both in this volume and in his booklet called *Conservation and the Countryside: By Quango or Market* (London: Institute of Economic Affairs, 1996) there is an alternative. The encouragement of private property rights works wonders for conservation in practice all over the world. Private nature reserves, deed restrictions and covenants can all be used to protect scenic views, habitats and open spaces. We need to rediscover competitive conservation entrepreneurs by allowing them to reward themselves for innovative schemes that benefit the environment. At present all the incentives point the other way: they penalise landowners with the most biodiverse habitats by loading them with designations and oppressive restrictions. Let those who improve their landscapes be rewarded with an alleviation of their regulatory burden, not an increase in it.

Individual property rights were the making of the English landscape over a thousand years. Why throw them away for a system of central planning that has proved so disastrous elsewhere?

Deregulating The Land:
An Alternative Route to Urban and Rural Regeneration

Mark Pennington

INTRODUCTION

GREATER REGULATION OF land use must, according to the current wisdom, lie at the heart of a strategy to stimulate the renaissance of urban areas and to preserve the integrity of the countryside. If market forces are allowed to operate freely, it is argued, then the core of the urban fabric will be decimated as the populace flees for the suburbs and the market towns and, in the process, destroys the rural idyll that it seeks. Such fears lie at the heart of the current government's 'sustainable development' agenda and would appear to underpin long-standing public support for policies such as the green belt. It is my contention, however, that far from alleviating these problems the system of land use regulation that prevails in the United Kingdom has often exacerbated the economic and social ills visited upon both town and country alike. Rather than our continuing the trend towards greater regulation, therefore, we may better serve the interests of both urban and rural areas by a fundamental *deregulation* of the market in land.

BRITISH LAND USE POLICY:
A CASE OF OVER-REGULATION?

The British land use planning system represents one of the most comprehensive systems of government land use regulation to be found anywhere in the Western world. Under the provisions of the 1947 Town and Country Planning Act and subsequent legislation, landowners have been required to obtain planning permission for all but very minor non-agricultural uses. In turn, the powers available under the planning system have enabled policymakers to pursue policies that have had a fundamental effect on the environments of both urban and rural areas.

Urban planning policy in Britain has long been dominated by a consistent emphasis on a strategy of urban containment. Through the designation of sites such as green belts, governments have sought to prevent the outward expansion of the cities and of migration to the countryside. In recent years the emphasis on this approach has been reinvigorated as part of the sustainable development agenda, which arose in the wake of the 1992 Earth Summit in Rio de Janeiro. It is now suggested that the planning system should act as a strategic device to encourage more 'sustainable' forms of urban living, discouraging the use of 'non-renewable' greenfield sites, and to concentrate development on 'brownfield' sites, regenerating urban areas and hence relieving the pressure for outward migration to the countryside.

Just as urban planning has been characterised by a regulation-intensive approach, so too has rural policy become dominated by a state-centred framework. On the one hand, the farming industry has been the recipient of enormous government largesse, by way of the CAP; and on the other, partly in exchange for such generosity, farmers and landowners have become subject to an ever greater array of government controls that determine the operations of the agricultural sector. Initially such controls were focused on farming operations themselves, but as public concern for environmental protection has mounted, controls have increasingly extended to the designation of special sites for the purposes of conservation.

The agenda sketched above constitutes a highly interventionist model of land use control. In theoretical terms there are strong arguments that can be advanced in favour of government regulation of the land market as a response to instances of 'market failure'. It is undoubtedly the case that land markets are prone to many imperfections, which allow both businesses and consumers to impose costs on the community without paying the social and environmental costs of so doing. The construction of urban developments on greenfield sites, for example, can lead to a loss of amenities such as scenic views, which are not taken into account by the developers and subsequent consumers. These are classic examples of the externalities and public goods problems that are the standard fare of micro-economic theory.

As is often the case in arguments over the merits of government intervention, however, there is an unfortunate tendency for those who advocate more regulation to compare the imperfect results that flow from the operation of the market with those of a fictional process of flawless bureaucratic administration. For governments to perform such a role would require that public sector officials be in possession of full information with regard to the pattern of public preferences, yet as the abysmal record of most government forecasting shows, this is rarely if ever the case. The argument for intervention is further diminished when it is recognised that governments, especially when they operate at the behest of special interest groups and the state bureaucracy itself, are themselves capable of imposing unwanted costs on groups who lack the organisational capacity to mobilise in the political system. In this case, the existence of government-generated externalities can be just as great as, if not greater than, those stemming from the private market.

While it would be imprudent to downplay the potential for market failure in land use, the experience of British land use policy does lead me to suspect that 'government failure' may be a critical issue. More specifically, there is reason to believe that *over-regulation* in both town and country alike has led to a decrease in the opportunities for both economic *and* environmental improvement. The frequent calls by environmentalists and planners for yet more state intervention and regulation are somewhat surprising in this context given that British land use policy for the last half-century has been *dirigiste* to the core. While some form of regulatory framework is always likely to be necessary there is evidence to suggest that many of today's most pressing planning problems are the product of *too much* and not too little regulation.

OVER-REGULATION IN THE CITIES

One of the most pressing concerns for contemporary land use policy has been the threat to the countryside posed by the migration of many urban dwellers to rural areas, and hence the rising demand for housing and other developments on greenfield sites. Policies such as green belts have been strengthened in order to stem this process and to redirect people back to the towns – the area of designated green belt, for example, more than doubled under the supposedly 'deregulating' Thatcher administration.

In order to understand why there are such strong pressures for development in the countryside, one must first appreciate why it is that people are indeed seeking to escape the towns. To some extent, population decentralisation can be accounted for by the fundamental shift away from city-based manufacturing industries towards much more mobile forms of service sector employment, which are able to operate from suburban and rural locations. In addition to these trends, however, there is evidence to suggest that the environmental conditions that pertain in the cities themselves have also constituted an important factor in encouraging people to migrate towards the country.

As noted above, a primary argument advanced in favour of policies such as the green belt is that by preventing development in the countryside and on the urban fringe, planning controls can help redirect economic activity back into the older urban areas, and hence relieve pressure on rural land. In actual fact, however, there are strong reasons to believe that policies of this nature may have precisely the opposite effect.

While it is true that increasing dwelling densities in cities still further may save *some* environmental amenities by stopping greenfield development on the urban fringe, it is also the case that environmental conditions in the towns and cities themselves may decline as urban congestion and pollution may worsen. Seen in this context, it may be the lack of such environmental amenities brought about by the *existing planning system* that is already encouraging people to escape the cities and to head for the less congested countryside. It may, therefore, be appropriate to allow at least some greenfield development on the edge of cities in order to avoid further congestion in the urban areas themselves. Allowing some development in the green belt would also help to lessen the so-called 'leap-frog' phenomenon, where development that is not permitted in the green belt itself, shifts instead to the 'deep' rural areas beyond. It is arguably this phenomenon which has been responsible for the massive expansion of rural market towns into the countryside that has occurred in recent years. The choice, therefore, should be seen not as one of encouraging a 'free for all', in which the entire countryside is concreted over (an unlikely event given that even in the heavily populated south-east 85% of the land area is presently in rural uses), but as one of allowing *some* development in the metropolitan green belts in order to alleviate pressure within the cities *and* in the deeper countryside beyond.

In addition to the problems of urban congestion, highlighted above, perhaps the major reason why people and businesses often wish to move to the countryside, and hence put pressure on rural land, is that urban local authorities and businesses have exhibited such a poor record in delivering the residential and shopping environments and other services (schools, crime prevention, etc.) that their residents prefer. Urban planning policies, epitomised either by mass public sector housing schemes or by substantial tracts of derelict local authority-owned land, have contributed to the degradation of many urban areas, a process that has shown only minor signs of reversal in recent years. Town centre shopping developments are, for example, often seen as dirty and inconvenient when compared to their out-of-town equivalents. Adopting a still more stringent emphasis on containment policies under these conditions may be equivalent to granting failing town centre businesses a monopoly market and urban local authorities monopolistic control over the local tax base. In these circumstances, without further competition from out-of-town or rural development, urban businesses and local authorities may have little incentive to improve the quality of services that they provide and to find more innovative ways of making urban environments attractive places in which to live.

It may even be argued that it is the relative lack of competition brought about by existing planning/containment policies that has perpetuated the lack of economic dynamism in the cities themselves. Urban areas that are already protected from competition by containment policies are prone to higher taxes, poor services and regulations that thwart the development of small businesses. Over-regulation in particular is a serious problem. In some of the poorest urban local authorities, where one would expect that development would be encouraged, the scale of the planning bureaucracy provides a severe check on economic development, especially from the small business sector. In authorities such as Lambeth, for example, fewer than 20% of planning applications are processed within the government target period of eight weeks. This is hardly the result of a lack of staff and resources. The average productivity of planning departments in urban Britain is less than two planning applications processed per month, per worker. In reality, local authority planners have no incentive to keep regulation down, because the more plans and regulations that must be completed, the greater the number of personnel employed in the department.

The problem of over-regulation in towns and cities, poor service provision and hence migration to the countryside is ultimately linked to the thorny issue of local government finance. Urban local authorities have precious few incentives to avoid over-regulation and to find innovative ways of making their cities attractive places in which to live because, for the most part, they are not responsible for raising their own revenue. On the contrary, the vast majority of services are funded through central government transfer payments. If local authorities fail to keep regulation down or to provide the services that their inhabitants desire, and if people leave the cities in response, the authority has insufficient incentive to win its tax base back. Rather, if authorities lose their tax base or fail in some other way, they then become eligible for still further central government subsidies and grants to make up any deficit and to engage in 'regeneration schemes'. In such cases, local authorities may often have a material interest in being chronically inefficient.

OVER-REGULATION IN THE COUNTRYSIDE

If economic and environmental conditions in the cities have been the victims of over-regulation, so too have those in the countryside. The land use planning system has, by and large, protected the countryside from the spread of urban developments – though at the cost of substantially higher house prices as those who flee the cities compete for the scarce supply of rural housing – but has failed to consider what the countryside is being preserved *for*. All too often, rural areas have been 'preserved' not for environmental purposes but for the continual expansion of subsidised farming – the alarming environmental consequences (loss of hedgerows, etc.) of which are now well known. Unfortunately, as recognition of the environmental effects of subsidised agriculture has become widespread, rather than seeking to remove the cause of the damage – i.e. to reduce agricultural subsidies – governments have responded by imposing a raft of regulatory controls on farmers and landowners. The designation, by bodies such as English Nature, of Sites of Special Scientific Interest and other such areas appears to have strong public support, yet it is far from clear that they represent the most appropriate way to encourage environmental protection.

One of the major failings of rural land use policy stems from the character of the incentives facing the bureaucrats in the nature conservation agencies themselves. While it should be recognised that some designated SSSIs and other such sites do indeed represent valuable habitats, which are in urgent need of protection, the priorities of the government bodies are heavily skewed towards the activity of site designation per se. Designating new sites requires site inspection, mapping, evaluation and documentation of 'potentially damaging practices' – all of which are extremely staff- and administration-intensive activities. It is not surprising, therefore, that over recent years the proportion of expenditure devoted to such regulatory activities has soared when compared to the monies that are actually used by farmers for conservation practices on the ground. Between 1981 and 1995 an extra 1,200 SSSIs were created in England and Wales, bringing the total to 3,800, or 7% of the land area. The ever-growing number of SSSIs is not, however, matched by a corresponding increase in the number of high-quality habitats. On the contrary, the more sites that are designated, the more devalued becomes the concept as the conservation bodies spend time and resources designating sites that are of increasingly doubtful environmental value.

Ironically, the further designation of such sites may actually be contributing to the diminution of environmental quality. If the countryside is to avoid being turned completely into a museum piece then it is imperative that farmers and landowners be allowed to find new ways of making a living from their land. Prime candidates for such an approach would be the development of leisure- and tourism-related activities. These developments would in many cases prove a more environmentally sensitive option than the agricultural uses that they might replace, the virtually invisible rural leisure developments supplied by firms such as Center Parcs being an important example in point. More often than not, however, such developments are ruled out of court by regulation and farmers are forced to maintain their land in agricultural practices simply *because* it is designated an SSSI or equivalent. As opportunities for commercial diversification are increasingly regulated out of existence, so farmers become more and more dependent on the maintenance of subsidised and environmentally damaging farm practices.

The economic options for farmers and landowners have been further reduced by more recent policies such as the proposed introduction of a statutory right to roam. As the vitriolic nature of debate on this issue has indicated, farmers and landowners have actively sought to prevent recreational users and walkers from entering their property for fear of damage to crops and for more general breaches of property rights (littering, vandalism, etc.). At present, the growing demand for recreational use of the countryside for walking and other leisure activities has been thwarted by the continued subsidisation of intensive agriculture. If, however, as a result of the world trade negotiations, agricultural protection under the CAP was to decline, then landowners would increasingly have an incentive to *attract recreational users on to their land, so long as they can charge a market price for doing so.* Unfortunately, however, the introduction of a right to roam is likely to stifle the development of such a commercial market in recreational access rights, because landowners will now be deprived of their property rights and of the right to charge for entrance. Members of the Ramblers Association or walkers in general are unlikely to be willing to pay for the recreational services that they are using if they have been guaranteed a state-sanctioned 'right' to enter 'free at the point of delivery'.

It should also be noted that the introduction of a right to roam is itself likely to be detrimental to environmental quality. By effectively removing the right of landowners to exclude recreational users from their property, such legislation is likely to create the conditions where a 'tragedy of the commons' scenario may emerge. In thinly populated countries such as Sweden, which have a long-established tradition of free access to uncultivated land, the environmental consequences of such policies have been minimal. Where population densities are low and pressure on resources is relatively light, 'open access regimes' may actually be the most appropriate institutional option, because the environmental costs of enforcing private property rights may not be sufficiently outweighed by the relevant benefits. In Britain, by contrast, with a substantially higher population-to-land ratio (six times the population of Sweden in half the land area) and much greater demand for recreational access, the environmental consequences are potentially far-reaching. Should recreational use begin to exceed levels that are compatible with conservation objectives, recreational users will have little incentive to modify their behaviour because they will not be required to pay a price for the environmental services that are being used. Meanwhile, landowners will continue to have little incentive to enhance environmental quality because they will be unable to capture the returns from so doing.

DEREGULATING THE LAND: SOME SUGGESTIONS FOR REFORM

The analysis presented above suggests that many of the ills facing both town and country are the result of an overly intrusive system of government land use regulation. On the one hand, the decline of the cities has been intensified by restrictive planning policies, while on the other the dependence of rural areas on environmentally damaging agricultural practices has been perpetuated by a regulatory process, the need for which was itself stimulated by a previously misguided intervention – the CAP. If over-regulation is the cause of such economic and environmental pathologies, then perhaps it is time to consider the possibility of a deregulation of the market in land in order to provide a cure.

Countryside protection and especially concerns over the spread of housing and other urban developments are clearly an important priority for the public and politicians alike, yet, as the analysis sketched in this chapter has shown, instruments such as green belts are often inappropriate to the task in hand. Paradoxical as it may seem, one way of protecting the heartland of rural Britain from the threat of urban sprawl would be to allow *a selective relaxation of green belt policy*. As noted earlier, green belts have in many ways been responsible for the growth of development pressure in and around the rural market towns. In this case, development which is forbidden in the urban green belt is simply forced out into the rural areas of the 'deep countryside' beyond (perhaps twenty to thirty miles out from the city centres). Contrary to popular opinion, green belts *do not* protect 'deep rural' areas, but are situated on the very edge of the major metropolitan areas and consist of land, especially in areas such as north-west England and parts of the London fringe, which is far from spectacular in terms of its aesthetic properties. Allowing development to occur in these 'brown belt' zones within the green belt would *act to alleviate the pressure for migration to more distant and more attractive rural locations*. As with all 'command and control' policies, green belts are not particularly sensitive to local variations in environmental conditions and, their name notwithstanding, may often result in a loss of environmental quality overall. A first step towards environmental improvement, therefore, would see an end to the blanket enforcement of green belt policy.

Second, allowing at least some development to take place in the green belt will also help to avoid the problem of over-congestion in the towns themselves. The current policy focus of trying to cram the vast majority of new development into existing urban areas is likely to be counter-productive, as the urban congestion and pollution that lead many people to leave the cities in the first place may actually worsen.

Third, a liberalisation of green-belt policy and the possibility of allowing more development on the urban fringe will provide a competitive stimulus to urban local authorities whose current monopoly power over their residents would be reduced. Maintaining a blanket emphasis on green belts allows many local authorities to get away with the provision of poor-quality services and urban environments because the options of escape for their residents (especially the poor and the unemployed) are so heavily constrained. Ultimately, more liberal planning policies would need to be combined with a fundamental reform of local government finance, returning revenue-raising powers to local authorities while cutting back on centrally raised taxes. Until towns and cities are faced with the need to win a tax base by avoiding over-regulation, providing better services and making their communities more attractive places in which to live, rather than relying on central government largesse, then the desire to flee to the countryside is more than likely to persist.

To impose a blanket ban on *all* greenfield development, as, for example, Simon Jenkins wants, is not a viable or just political option. To forbid any housing development on greenfield sites would be to condemn the urban population to an ever more congested and polluted environment and to cause a massive rise in the price of housing, which would force many families out of the housing market altogether. A relaxation of inappropriate green belt policies by contrast, could, as argued above, contribute to the improvement of environmental quality in the cities (by reducing congestion) and reduce the pressure for housing development in the rural heartlands beyond the green belt.

Turning to the 'deep rural' areas, farmers and landowners should be given much more latitude to use the environmental qualities of the countryside and to turn them into a viable economic asset. It is fallacious to claim, as many environmentalists do, that private landowners represent a threat to countryside conservation and that greater state regulation will end this threat. In so far as farmers and landowners have been responsible for environmental failure, this has largely been a product of their responding to incentives provided by the *existing system of state intervention* – namely the massive levels of agricultural support that have characterised the past fifty years. Abolish such subsidies and rural landholders would have a positive incentive *to attract people on to their land for leisure- and recreation-based activities*. In this sense, the environmental attributes of the countryside are one of the greatest economic assets that landowners possess. In order for the potential of these assets to be realised, however, it is essential that the property rights of landowners be maintained, so that they may properly capture the commercial benefits of conservation activities. To this end, proposals for a statutory right to roam should be abandoned and existing regulatory controls that limit the commercial development of tourism and leisure-related activities should be relaxed.

The measures sketched above should, of course, be seen as only the start of a much longer-term objective of moving towards a more market-oriented system of land use control. Experience throughout the world, and confirmed in the British case, suggests that centralised bureaucratic planning reduces incentives for innovation and change, and prevents people from adapting to the local environmental conditions that they face. In the longer term, therefore, the aim of public policy should be to assign private property rights to a wider array of environmental assets and hence facilitate the development of a functioning market. As incomes rise with economic growth there will be an ever-rising demand for recreational access to the countryside and for developments that are sensitive to the aesthetic qualities of the countryside. Property rights approaches will provide incentives for landowners and farmers to respond to this rising demand by providing them with the capacity to reap commercial benefits from the maintenance of environmental quality.

For a more comprehensive analysis of the British planning system and for information about sources, readers should consult M. Pennington, *Planning and the Political Market: Public Choice and the Politics of Government Failure* (London: Athlone Press, 2000).

A MANAGED LANDSCAPE

Alan Kilkenny

LANDSCAPE THAT IS truly natural is now only rarely seen in these densely populated islands of ours. There are few examples left in Britain of wilderness – of countryside that does not bear witness to the mark of man.

In some cases the hand of man is obvious – tarmac, concrete and fields of ordered crops. Elsewhere he has shown a lighter, but no less significant touch. Indeed, so harmonious has his involvement been that many now view the largely man-made landscape as the epitome of the natural world. But what precisely has man done to change the work of nature?

In addition to the impact of buildings, roads, railways and the planting of crops, he has altered the course of rivers, and has drained marshland and river margins. He has taken down woodland, planted forests, enclosed land, domesticated wild animals, created pasture, introduced alien species and subverted the food chain. He has laid siege to weeds and insects, checked predation and manicured the land from hillside to river bottom. He has created habitats on the grand scale and on the miniature.

Every landscape has its own distinct features. The shape of the land, its surface water and its vegetation lays testament to the underlying rock and its regolith, indicating drainage, soil type and fertility.

Enclosure is perhaps man's first and most obvious contribution, the framework of hedges, fences, walls and dykes which sets out the structure of the patchwork.

This image of the countryside, this bucolic idyll, is firmly implanted in the minds of our now largely urban population. Unfortunately for the rural dweller, there is no room for man within the picture. This is theme park countryside.

The reality of course is that man enters the picture every day, and not just to pick up the rubbish after the visitors have gone home. There is little of our landscape that would remain so beautiful if he were to withdraw from the scene. As we have seen from the visual horror that is set-aside, cultivated land is not a pretty sight once nothing is planted in it. Hedges that are not maintained soon lose their charm, as well as their definition.

It has been many centuries since returning to nature was an option. The natural world in Britain no longer exists, and we could not recreate it. The landscapes that we hold so dear are inextricably bound up with the economic life and social pastimes of rural man. These have of course evolved over time, and those changes have been reflected in the landscape, often for the better, but not always.

Landscape in Britain has never been ossified, nor should it be. It will continue to evolve, but the speed and desirability of change will depend in large part on the value which society as a whole attaches to the rural way of life, and the price which it is prepared to pay to sustain it.

Is it appropriate, even if it were affordable, to countenance, and indeed to encourage, the production of food and timber in places where such production is profoundly non-competitive in terms of price, or quality, or both? Self-sufficiency is an increasingly difficult argument to sustain in a stable world with sophisticated transport and communications. Farmers and growers operate within a marketplace which is both very large and very efficient.

Producers will be increasingly obliged to play to their strengths, either as paradigms of efficiency or as specialists. The omens for landscape are clear – less diversity and, unless some acceptable means can be devised to keep people on the hills, farmers and growers retreating altogether from the most marginal areas of production.

At first sight, all of this bodes ill for the nation's favourite landscape, which depends for its existence upon traditional mixed farming. Salvation may, however, be at hand in the shape of the organic movement.

Organic farms depend upon mixed farming practices, and it is clear that public demand will require ever more organic produce, whether on the stalls at farmers' markets or on the supermarket shelves. But there are those who suggest that organic food is no better for us than food produced with the aid of chemicals.

I for one long for the day when juggernauts laden with chemicals are no longer to be seen edging their way into British farmyards, and when the breeze is tainted with nothing more noxious than the smell of muck. Provided that organic food is in nutritional terms no worse for us to eat, then the emotional, economic and environmental advantages render indisputable the case for organic production.

This is a major challenge, and there is no inexpensive solution. If we like the way our countryside looks, and if we do not want to lose it, we must be prepared to pay the price necessary to maintain it.

One solution might be to offer financial rewards for those living and working in designated areas who are prepared to maintain the fabric of the landscape which we treasure. This would be not be a hand-out from the state, nor income support by another name. This would be payment for services rendered.

Defining the basis and the standards against which payments would be made would be kept as simple as possible, with administration to match. The scheme needs to be straightforward, transparent and unambiguous, with rewards sufficient only to make the difference between staying or going.

No doubt such a scheme would be accompanied by calls for greater access to land so rewarded. At the same time, we should also consider asking those who wish to enjoy the countryside to pay a little towards its upkeep. In the same way that Britain's millions of fishermen must all pay for and carry a rod licence, perhaps we should be considering a duty on cagoules!

Woodland in general, and cover in particular, including hedgerows, is often maintained in the face of all economic sense. Those who choose to adopt this course do so freely, and at no cost to the taxpayer. They do it simply for the love of the countryside and in most cases for the love of their sport.

Their actions have a profoundly positive effect upon habitat and wildlife, and add enormously to landscape throughout Britain. The removal of hunting, shooting and fishing would not only result in the decline of wildlife, it would accelerate the process of landscape change, and in a way most of us would consider highly undesirable.

There are vivid and painful examples only just across the North Sea of the outcome for the countryside of decisions born out of a failure of understanding and driven through by political dogma. In the Netherlands, for instance, where shooting was banned some years ago, disease and comprehensive neglect have followed. Predation of ground-nesting birds has increased dramatically, pushing some species to the brink of extinction.

We have allowed the town and the countryside to drift far apart. The chasm of mutual mistrust and misunderstanding is wide, and meaningful debate is rare. Yet the countryside is unquestionably a national resource. It is indeed a countryside for all. It must still be there for our children and grandchildren to enjoy, just as we have enjoyed it. But country people alone do not have the power, even if they had the resources, to protect its future.

The nation as a whole will, consciously or otherwise, determine the future of the countryside and of those who live there. We must be sensitive to the views of those for whom the countryside is a place of relaxation rather than employment. At the same time, it places a considerable duty on the visitor to act with equal responsibility, and to display a willingness to understand and a preparedness to respect country ways.

As a nation, we need to establish the true value that we place on our countryside. As a nation, we need to establish whether we are prepared to meet its true cost.

Landscape is usually at its best when left untouched by man or when sensitively managed by him. The commercial pressures on farming and the financial pressures on many rural dwellers are such that profound, and potentially unmanaged, change in the landscape is close at hand.

There are too many examples within Britain and beyond of man's greed or negligence ruining a landscape, often forever. What is clear is that change, just like the landscape itself, has to be managed.

THE FARM OF THE FUTURE

FARMING AND THE CAP

John Gummer

TODAY'S MEALTIMES: SNACKING IS KING

MANY IN THE rich world, who do not blanch at forking out
£30,000 for a more fashionable motor car, will refuse to
expend threepence more on a fresher lettuce or a tastier loaf
of bread. Food, which ought to rank highest among our
spending priorities, has been relegated to the rank of a
necessity, and in this advanced civilisation of ours, only
luxuries deserve to be prized. We take necessaries as our right
and expect them to be delivered at a discount.

So it is that food prices demand a smaller and smaller proportion of a prosperous household's income and take less
time than ever for the average worker to earn. What is more,
now that packaging, distribution and preparation are
necessary on-costs, the basic food content of what we buy
represents an even smaller proportion of what we pay. With
one in three meals eaten out of the home and most of the rest
to a growing extent pre-prepared, that proportion will
continue to fall.

Even our habits of eating have contributed to this change in
the place of food in our lives. Fewer and fewer families sit
down at a table to eat together, even at the weekend. Dietary
fads and the mother's surrender to the refrigerator have
meant that increasingly each member of the family caters
differently for their needs. Working mothers choose not to
cook for all and life for the young is led to a much greater

extent outside the home. So a vegetarian, slimming daughter on a diet buys the ready-prepared offering that promises she will lose weight, while her teenage brother indulges whatever eating preferences he happens to have, and both eat at whatever intervals suit their mood. Snacking is king. We advanced nations have ceased to take our meals in common and have descended to sequential grazing.

TODAY'S FARMERS: CREATURES OF THE INTERNATIONAL TRADER

Food choice therefore increasingly moves away from the farmer. The importance of the individual grower, the choice of variety, the care in husbandry, and the competence and flair count less and less. Instead the farmer is expected to provide a standardised commodity meeting the specifications of the major buyers. Differentiation is the business of the factory and the packager. At the margin, of course, there are counter-indications. Farmers' markets, organic production, full traceability and welfare concerns all link back to the primary producer. Yet these are the preoccupations of the few, even among the French! For the vast majority, food has been detached from those who produce it and prices reflect that indiscrimination. The farmers of the industrialised world have become what their tropical cousins have been for so long, the creatures of the international trader. Wheat, maize and oil seeds, beef, lamb and chicken, have joined coffee, cocoa and palm oil to require industrial commodity production, not agriculture in the traditional European sense. They have become our cash crops and their purchasers have no more interest in the rural conditions in which they are produced than they have in the implications for the social structure of Washington New Town when they buy a Hitachi television. The international market in foodstuffs demands industrial attitudes and business concerns whose operatives are thought to have no more role in their local community than any other technical employee. Thus the commercial logic of modern agriculture flies in the face of the social and environmental demands of farming and the countryside.

RURAL MYTH vs. REAL COUNTRYSIDE

Yet we insist that it is otherwise. We ask of our farmers that they care for the countryside, take their traditional part in village life, promote conservation, uphold high standards of animal welfare, and maintain the rural myth that urban people remember from the stories of their childhood. That myth retains a strong hold even in societies like the British that are long removed from their agricultural roots. Unfortunately it gives rise to a view of the countryside far divorced from reality. Indeed divorced not just from today's realities but from those of yesterday as well. It idealises farming with its chickens in the farmyard and the jolly farmer ploughing his small fields and the dairymaid caring for the cows she knows by name. How different from monoculture with its vast fields and huge tractors that apply fertiliser differentially with phenomenal accuracy, guided by the satellite positioning devices installed in air-conditioned cabs.

Even in France, where society is happily much closer to the land, the emotional view of the rural world is increasingly out of date. There are few French townspeople without pretty close connection to the countryside. Their urban transformation came much later than ours. Nonetheless today's farming is very different from that remembered from afar. The village, deep in the Auvergne, where I lived for many of my childhood summers, had seven farming families, each tending a few cows and sheep, making local cheese and selling a few cash crops. Now there are none. The land is deserted. The farms, where once the cows were housed below and the families above, are now all converted into weekend and holiday homes, adorned with neat shutters and hanging baskets of flowers.

Yet, although even in France working villages have become rural retreats, the image in the town dweller's mind is still that of the rugged peasant tearing a poor living from an unyielding soil: an image that evokes real sympathy.

It is no wonder, therefore, that we find agricultural issues so difficult to handle. The free-market philosophy is riding triumphant – even into mercantilist France. We therefore look to see in agriculture all the requirements of the market-driven system: competition, economies of scale, agglomeration, standardisation and globalisation. We demand free trade, worldwide competition and farmers who stand on their own feet without support or subsidy. At the same time, the rural myth exercises its powerful pull. We half accept that farmers need support and yet we have no clearly defined philosophy as to why.

AGRICULTURE'S NEW ISOLATION

Once it was simpler. We needed to safeguard our food supplies. The feeling was even stronger in a continental Europe that had such recent memories of starvation. It was also a much more powerful traditional theme there. Germany's fixed policy of high grain prices to protect its farmers stretched back before Bismarck. Indeed the key reason that Austria was not allowed into the *Zollverein* was that it did not conform to that requirement. So there's nothing new about the attitude. What is new is the loss of fear. The fall of the Soviet Union has removed the fear of war and long-term over-production has removed the fear of shortage. That absence of fear destroys the rationale for subsidies.

THE WTO'S IMPACT

Agriculture is therefore newly isolated today. That isolation is not confined to the UK. It is a growing fact in much of the rest of Europe, although one that is not yet reflected in the rhetoric of the farm ministers! Nonetheless, what is happening psychologically is paralleled by political events. The WTO has already changed fundamentally the future course of subsidies. By capping and containing them, by prohibiting new trade distorting support, by insisting upon access to markets, by limiting the scope of support and by outlawing particular mechanisms, the WTO has had a significant impact. That impact is growing. Partly that is because these measures, agreed in the Uruguay Round, take some time to come into force. Partly too it is because, in the limbering up for the next round, all sides are recognising that further and more radical changes to the subsidies system are going to be inevitable.

No participant in the WTO talks is more central to all this than the EU. In essence, the trade organisation is dominated by the two world players – the USA and the EU. It is of course perfectly true that everyone who is a member has an equal right to speak and participate. It is also true that the G7 and the free-trade enthusiasts, led by Australia and such countries as Argentina, have real influence. Nonetheless, in the end, it is America and Europe that have to do the deal and it is they who make the real decisions. On its own, no single country can wield much influence, save in very special circumstances as obtained when the USA insisted on challenging the Japanese attitude to rice imports during the last round. Otherwise no single nation plays any really effective part in the decision-making process. It is as a part of the EU that the UK has been able to be a pivotal player in this process.

That was particularly true in the Uruguay Round when the UK had the presidency. At the time, I chaired the Agriculture Council and was able to help form a positive position for the EU in which we could safeguard the environmental payments to farmers and keep them out of the categories of support that would be banned or restricted. Happily for British agriculture, the more sensitive attitudes of continental governments had also to be taken into account. Thus the determination of the UK to move further towards free trade was not bought at the expense of farmers as would have been the case had we had entirely our own way. On the other hand, our leadership ensured that the intransigence of the French in particular could be softened sufficiently to make an agreement possible.

Yet again that experience was most revealing. Despite the free-trade rhetoric, the USA subsidises its farmers to a very considerable extent. It is also ruthless in manipulating other mechanisms to protect them from competition. Every difficulty is put in the way of exporters to the USA. The powerful lobbying of the well-financed commodity groups ensures that these systems continue and that the WTO rules are written in such a way that they catch the Europeans while excluding the USA. Environmentally-based subsidies are imperilled because they are of little interest to the USA, whose agricultural support is essentially of the pork barrel variety. It is elicited from government, both at the state and federal level, by electoral pressure. They are buying votes with little attempt at further excuse.

DEALING WITH THE PROBLEM OF AGRICULTURE
The Problem's Apparent Intractability

It is therefore not surprising that in an increasingly globalised world, the problem of agriculture seems intractable. In the UK there is not a sufficient sentiment among the urban majority to provide an effective voice for support. In the EU more widely, the change from production subsidies that are increasingly outlawed, to environment packages that are not, is slow and unstructured. In the world, the pressures for free trade have not yet been countered by an effective alternative subsidy system that would attract support from the two groups that count – the USA and the EU. At no level have we a way forward that commands a consensus.

A Solution: Make Environmental Payments
Central to Support

It seems therefore almost hubristic even to propose a solution. Yet I do believe that there is one to hand that ought to be attainable. It builds upon the British experience of environmental payments, not just because they address the real problem of land management but because they provide the justification of subsidy that commands the most widespread support. At the moment these payments are marginal – perhaps 5% of the total subsidy bill in the UK. Yet, in other countries where the politics demand that more be done for farmers, that percentage is growing. If recently proposed changes in France are adopted, then environmentally modulated payments will constitute nearly 20% of the total bill.

Britain has led the way in imaginative schemes to deliver environmental benefits but has never been prepared to spend enough on spreading them more widely so that they do become a central part of our agricultural support. This failure is directly attributable to the Treasury, which neither understands rural issues nor wishes to.

Coping with the Treasury

No department of government outside the DETR and MAFF has much interest in the countryside but the Treasury seems positively to glory in its ignorance. That is partly because it is more convenient to assume that farming ought to be an industry like any other and partly because the whole system of agricultural support is very complex and the Treasury has never seen fit to master it. Indeed I remember one Chief Secretary who, after the usual jousting that was an essential part of the annual spending round, called me to the Treasury and said, 'Look, John, there is no way that either I or my officials are ever going to understand the Common Agricultural Policy as you do, so let's just agree on the level of the cuts I want and I'll leave it to you to see where you can get them.' It was a piece of flattery not to be fallen for, but behind it lay more truth than those officials would like to admit. They just feel less in control when it comes to the arcane business of agriculture than when they deal elsewhere. There is, besides, a real fear of being landed with expenditure that cannot be gainsaid or restrained. The only parallel is Defence but even then there is none of the complication of Europe-wide decision-making nor the effect of the interaction between a Green Pound and a soft Euro.

So it is that a more than ordinarily suspicious Treasury, with an ingrained belief that agricultural support is, of its nature, unacceptable, refuses to countenance the kind of changes that would swing our spending firmly towards environmental payments. It has no interest in making subsidies acceptable and the more intolerable the CAP is seen to be, the more it suits its ultimate goal – the eradication of agricultural support. Even when the question is not of additional UK spending but a shift Europe-wide, the Treasury demands significant reduction in the totals as its price for supporting change. It will not accept the inevitable fact that there is no appetite among our partners for beggaring their farmers. It may be that the demands of the WTO and their own public opinion is forcing an increasing willingness to consider different, and more environmentally acceptable, ways of directing the support, but that doesn't mean cuts. That opportunity for change is there for us to seize but it isn't going to deliver huge savings.

And there is the rub. British farmers miss out on many of the sensible environmental payments offered by the EU because they are discretionary. Taking up such payments reduces the British rebate. And so it should! Mrs Thatcher argued that the UK paid in more to the EU budget and got out less. The arrangement she set up therefore links the rebate with the amount we take from EU funds. If the Treasury could manage it, farmers would take nothing and our rebate would then rise accordingly! In fact the mandarins cannot touch the majority of payments because they are obligatory. However, they can veto discretionary spending. So our farmers get a worse deal than their competitors in the rest of Europe. In effect, part of the rebate comes directly out of their pockets. Worse, we lose some payments designed to encourage environmentally friendly farming, organic production and small enterprises. Britain is therefore the European nation least likely to help its own agriculture from national funds and most likely to restrict access to EU funds. So, however creative we may be in the design of schemes that protect and enhance the countryside, they are always doomed to be only marginal through lack of funds to develop them more widely.

We have therefore the galling spectacle of versions of our Environmentally Sensitive Area scheme being taken up by others in a far more widespread and effective manner, while we squabble over every last penny spent on improving and enhancing the countryside. It is this that made us so ineffective in the unresolved debate over the reform of the CAP. We have pursued the urban agenda of reducing dramatically the overall cost, instead of a rural agenda of redirecting the support so that it sustains and enhances the countryside.

Reforming the CAP to Enhance the Countryside

Farmers have to make a living. The present system is impoverishing them and they are, for the first time, ready for radical change. Industrial farming could and should make its way on the world market without production support. However, that would leave much of the countryside untended and some of our most beautiful man-made landscapes would be destroyed. Without sheep on the uplands and cattle in the marshes, much of what we know as rural England would go. Properly managed crops and effective animal husbandry play an essential part in keeping this green and pleasant land.

The rest of Europe shares this common interest in our common environment. There is no future in demanding a repatriation of the CAP that would only drive every nation into agricultural competition of the very sort that would make environmental policies even more difficult. We need to protect the countryside that is our common inheritance. Given our small size, this is even more important for the UK than for the rest of the EU. We can expect little support from governments of any complexion. Repatriation merely puts the countryside into the hands of the British Treasury.

So what should we be seeking in the coming reforms? First, we should recognise our partners' concern about size. They have a real desire to support small farms, not just for electoral and social reasons but because of growing desertification. They want to see to it that farming in the Black Forest, the Ardeche and the Alto Adige is still possible. We have opposed special help for the small farmer because, when measured in absolute terms, so few of ours come into that category. The answer surely is to adopt a proportional approach. There should be particular help aimed at those whose enterprise falls among the bottom 20% of the *national* average. This would help us to provide effective payments which, among other things, would reduce stocking levels in Wales and Scotland, as well as in Cumbria and Yorkshire. We could keep farmers in the highlands without encouraging the over-grazing that is now so destructive. Elsewhere, there would at least be some slowing of the loss of the small family farm and a little more opportunity to keep more families in the countryside. It could never be sufficient to reverse the trend but it would help to hold it for those who do want to continue.

Second, we should sign up fully to the idea of cross-compliance. Those who want support must show that they are farming in an environmentally friendly way. Increasingly CAP payments would be decoupled from production and instead be available in respect of land management that enhanced the countryside. In the transition period farmers would be given incentives to produce in a less damaging way.

Third, we should increase the support for organic agriculture, particularly for conversion. This would include a radical realignment of our research budget that would enable work to be done on such issues as weed control and animal disease prevention that are such difficulties within the organic system. At the moment the UK market has to rely upon importing as much as 70% of its product – much of it indeed from outside Europe.

Fourth, we should extend the principles of the Environmentally Sensitive Area so that they cover the whole country. Any farmer ought to be able to enter into a contract with MAFF under which that farm, its land, crops and animals would be looked after in a way that enhances the countryside. Different levels of agreement should be available but all would seek to compensate the farmer for the return sacrificed by keeping hedgerows, planting wildlife strips, maintaining the water levels and stocking at appropriate densities.

Lastly, we should be able to be much more rapid in our response to new opportunities. Further research and support for the use of biomass and oil seeds for energy would be very timely, now that oil prices have again risen so rapidly. After all, we once grew all the fuel our farms needed when so much of the land was given over to the cultivation of oats for horses. The seriousness of our dependence upon regimes as alien as that of Saudi Arabia ought to make this a matter of increasing national concern. Opportunities for diversification can be much more effectively encouraged and the removal of perverse subsidies hastened. A war on fraud could properly be coupled with a range of national measures to give tax encouragement to small farm enterprises, holiday lettings and bed-and-breakfast, farm shops, farmers' markets and cottage industries. The most effective way of enhancing the countryside is to ensure that it continues to be a workplace and is not entirely given over to weekenders. The new CAP ought to have that aim firmly in mind. All over Europe, farmers are leaving the land at unprecedented rates. We need to ensure that there is at least some replacement of jobs that will attract and retain younger people. Otherwise large areas will be desertified or become home only to the rich and the retired.

Now, none of these solutions is revolutionary. It is just that they have been talked about, piloted, tested, but never properly tried. All of them can be made WTO-proof and each contributes to the creation of a countryside that fits the real demands of all our citizens. The enthusiasm that has replaced the initial wariness of the Environmentally Sensitive Area schemes shows that farmers too relish the opportunity to farm in a way that makes their surroundings so much more attractive. The skill and effort demanded soon removes the fear that this condemns real men and women to 'toy-town' agriculture.

Modulating the arrangements so that they fit the varying circumstances throughout Europe, without sacrificing the strength that comes from a common policy, gives the reform the necessary local sensitivity while protecting the universality that ensures that it can be argued through the WTO. It also provides the basis for a policy that is applicable to the new countries that will join the EU during the next five years. The present CAP is untenable in an enlarged Europe. These reforms could be the basis of a flexible common approach to agriculture in the world's largest trading grouping. At home they will enable us to resolve our agricultural dilemma. Our farmers will continue to produce food but they will have to choose either to compete in the international market place through becoming the most efficient of operators, or to produce in a way that enables them better to care for the countryside and to be supported by the community they thus serve. That support will have to be sufficient to make their stewardship financially possible.

The Treasury will not gain by the change but at least it will not lose, because spending can properly be capped, not least to protect us from the still immeasurable impact of the new entrants.

Paying the Farmer to Protect the Land

So, too, the public will know that what it spends has a very clear result. The rural advantages it craves could be delivered in a cost-effective manner and properly justify the taxpayers' support upon which they depend. They would be paying the farmer for doing what only the farmer can do: looking after the land and protecting the landscape that over the centuries farmers have created. In this way, we shall have marked out a course for farming in the new century that does not depend on increasingly contradictory attitudes towards agriculture. Instead we shall have clearly defined the kind of countryside we want to preserve and enhance and for which we are prepared to pay.

AN ORGANIC BLUEPRINT

Colin Spedding

ORGANIC FARMING HAS been with us for a long time. But only in the past five years has the debate about its ultimate value intensified. The area of UK land being farmed organically has risen rapidly from some 50,000ha at the end of 1996 to 425,000ha by the end of 1999. This represents more than 2% of agricultural land but only about 0.6% was fully converted. Most of the land is towards the south and west and Scotland.

There are few neutrals on what has become, quite unnecessarily, a battlefield. On the one hand, it is claimed that organic farming is the only safe and sensible way to farm; and, on the other, that it cannot feed the world and is largely a con trick based on unsupported claims, especially in relation to food safety.

It is worth examining these two extreme positions in more detail.

THE ORGANIC FARMERS

Organic enthusiasts are of two quite different kinds. The pioneer producers, long before there was any central control or European regulation, banded together in like-minded groups such as the Biodynamic Association and the Soil Association, convinced that this was a better way to farm. The emphasis was on the soil as the living basis for production, and on natural processes. This meant that artificial inputs had no (or only a very minor) place, which limited the levels of productivity and thus, for example, the levels of stocking density of livestock.

Intensive farming, as we know it today, simply could not happen within the organic approach. Present-day organic farmers now oppose intensive farming anyway; they see it as exploitative; it is not consistent with organic principles, and it affects soil organisms, the qualities of the product and animal welfare.

These original organisations were formed by people who wanted to farm in this way. They were not especially market-oriented, although they believed that their produce was 'better' in almost all senses.

The second kind of enthusiasts are those consumers who are convinced that the produce is better for them and, importantly, their children. They believe that organic food tastes better and is more nutritious as well as 'safer'. This group has grown enormously in recent years. Many consumers have become very concerned about excessive use of agrochemicals (mainly herbicides and pesticides but also drugs in livestock production) and, most recently, worries exemplified by BSE.

They believe that organically produced food is less likely to carry any of these risks. Since some such risks cannot necessarily be known – as BSE was not known to us before it became a major problem – there can be no guarantee of this. Furthermore, crops cannot be guaranteed to be free from spray-drift from neighbouring farms. However, they are perceived, reasonably, as less likely to be contaminated since the chemicals of major concern are not actually used in the course of production.

Those on the opposite side see such fears as unsubstantiated. They are angered by the implications that conventional farming is producing unsafe foods that may 'poison' the consumer. The 'organic' label claims only that the food has been produced according to the agreed standards, whereas enthusiasts claim all kinds of qualities for the food itself. The latter are not always based on good scientific evidence. How could any such evidence allow generalisations about all organic food versus all conventionally produced food?

I believe that any either/or proposition is nonsense. We do not have to choose between two extreme views as if one were right and the other wrong: it is entirely possible for both to be wrong.

Indeed, many people would favour an intermediate position, combining the best of both worlds, notably the more 'natural' methods of organic farming with the productivity and lower costs of conventional production.

TO FEED THE WORLD

One simplistic argument says that organic farming could not feed the world, especially in view of rapid population growth. But we already fail to feed the world, because the hungry and undernourished lack the money to buy food. If they had the money, the food would be delivered to them.

The Western world has been over-producing and is now taking active steps to reduce production, because there is no economic demand for their surpluses. How to feed is not the same question as how to produce enough food: surpluses and starvation have coexisted for years – even within one country.

Even if organic farming could not produce enough food, that does not mean that organic farming has no role at all. The issue is what this role should be, on what scale, and what would be the costs and benefits.

WHAT COULD ORGANIC FARMING OFFER TO THE COUNTRYSIDE?

Advocates of organic farming bring two charges against current arrangements which favour conventional farming. The first is that they are based on an inadequate cost-benefit analysis. In any proper calculation *all* the costs need to be included. Organic farmers would argue that many of the costs to society of conventional farming methods – nitrate pollution of rivers, reduction of biodiversity, environmental damage, the costs of subsidies – are never paid by conventional farmers. Second, insofar as conventional farming is implicated in the development of genetically modified crops and even animals, which is unpopular with the public, this gives the countryside a bad image.

In broad terms, the benefits to the countryside of organic farming are of three kinds: to the rural economy, to the structure and appearance of the countryside, and to its image.

First, there could be an increase in rural employment, mainly through the generation of jobs in local 'added-value' processing and local direct marketing, rather than just by greatly increased employment on the farms.

Relatively few extra jobs are created on organic farms, except perhaps in livestock rearing, though more labour is certainly needed per unit of output. But organic farmers would prefer to seek local outlets for their produce and to expand into processing and marketing locally. Different skills and a different order of management are needed to co-ordinate such a food chain.

Second, there would be benefits to the appearance of the countryside due to smaller fields, more hedges, etc. But these could only be significant if organic farming occupied much more than the current c. 3% of the farmland. However, the benefits to wildlife numbers and diversity are real and nothing about organic farming says it can operate only on a small scale: big organic farms – though probably not fields – are quite feasible.

Surveys of organic farms generally show a greater number and variety of wild birds and the invertebrates they feed on, as well as some small mammals. Even on large farms, fields are small and thus field boundaries (including hedges) are greater in length, and very often such boundaries provide wildlife refuges and corridors. By and large, pest numbers are controlled by predators and parasites but weed problems are more difficult.

That is not to say that conventional farms cannot – or do not already – provide similar benefits or that they could not be encouraged to do more. Some would argue that such developments would contribute, in total, vastly more, because of the greater areas involved, than organic farming will ever do. Others point out that the conservation of wildlife is an essential component of organic farming and not an optional extra that only some conventional farmers will embrace.

Environmental benefits are not exclusive to organic farming but they are built into its system, whereas conventional farming adds them on only if the individual farmer is interested or gets a grant to do so.

The third kind of benefit relates to the impact of organic farming on the image of the countryside, particularly as perceived by the urban majority. This rests on the inbuilt requirements that organic farming should include high standards of animal welfare (and the evidence is that it does), care of natural features (including stone walls and hedges), the idea of 'working with nature' and even concern for the people involved. This image could be of great importance in the town versus country debate.

It is not often realised that high standards of animal welfare are a requirement laid down in all Organic Production Standards. It is illegal to use the word 'organic' (or its equivalent in any EU member countries) on any food product unless it is produced according to these standards and the producer or processor is registered with (and inspected by) one or other of the six organic sector bodies licensed to operate in the UK. Their authority derives from their registration with the UK Register of Organic Food Standards (UKROFS), which is the designated body for the UK under EU regulation.

But there is also a general improvement in animal welfare in conventional farming as a result of the development of assurance schemes, greatly encouraged in the UK by very powerful retailers.

THE FUTURE OF ORGANIC FARMING

What, then, of the future?

Clearly, the demand for organic food, some of it based on fears and concern about food safety, is increasing and this is likely to continue, particularly if organic producers (and retailers) can live with lower prices.

Many more people say that they would buy organic produce if the price premium was not so large. On the other hand, costs generally remain higher for organic farming and these have to be met. But while volumes are small, there are also greater costs in retailing and these can be reduced if the volumes increase. So as demand increases and organic farming gains experience and skills, there should be scope for cost and price reduction.

Of course, meeting increasing demand has to take account of the stringent requirements imposed by the Organic Food Standards, including that of a conversion period of at least two years. During the conversion period productivity falls while the system is changed and no premiums are available because the products cannot yet be described as 'organic'.

The organic sector is highly regulated (under the EU regulation). The organic farm's label says only that the food has been produced to high (and accessible) standards: it is the customer who makes the link between the qualities of the product and the way in which it was produced. So the sector is likely to increase in area, numbers of people and range of products.

With more government support, more of the demand for organic foodstuffs could be met from home production. Currently over 70% is imported and most other European countries have already developed rather greater capacity, of land and farmers, than is available in the UK.

The development of organic farming here is impeded by several factors. Organic farming generally involves mixed farming and thus depends on outlets for livestock products, usually in relatively small numbers and preferably local. The disappearance of small abattoirs imposes insoluble problems of cost, transport and volume that could greatly constrain the development of the organic sector. Such closures would be disastrous. But it is not only the organic sector that would be affected: there are even wider implications to the rural economy.

There are good reasons to encourage organic farming in the interests of a thriving and attractive countryside but there is no point in trying to do this if there is no market for the produce or no profit for the farmer.

The future development of the organic sector is therefore inevitably an economic question. If unaided organic farming were profitable, there would be no problem in the sector's growing. Its current profitability depends largely on substantially higher prices but these probably limit demand.

Could organic farming survive a significant reduction in these prices? Opinions vary but greater technical efficiency should make it possible for organic farmers to succeed with lower prices for their products.

If more organic produce were available, the retail costs would be reduced. Handling and selling small quantities always costs more.

Advocates of organic farming believe it should be publicly supported for environmental reasons. But costing environmental harms and benefits is notoriously difficult. For example, the idea that conventional use of fertilisers causes nitrate pollution of watercourses, whereas organic farming does not, would be extremely difficult to quantify.

At present the government funds conversion to organic methods, arguing that this is not a subsidy but a recognition of the extra costs involved. Are substantial increases both possible and justified? There are some dangers in too rapid an increase in the number of organic farmers.

A reasonable aim would be an increase within the likely demand for products (and not all those imported could be home-produced) so that a genuine choice was available to both consumers and producers.

An organic sector of significant size – much greater than the current position – would have several important benefits. First, it would allow everyone to learn about the problems of larger-scale organic farming and about how they might be solved. Second, some of these solutions might also help conventional farmers to reduce their dependence on expensive and, in some cases, undesirable inputs. Third, much better economic comparisons could be made and the greater volume of production would encourage the development of retail outlets. Fourth, environmental benefits would be easier to quantify and the impact on landscape could be more easily assessed. But the fifth and most important benefit would be to people's quality of life, whether as consumers or producers, by increasing the ability to exercise choice.

REINVENTING AGRICULTURE

Graham Harvey

WALKING AROUND THE aisles of a modern supermarket it's not hard to see why shoppers forget about British agriculture's origins in the land and about the people who work it.

Perfect, blemish-free vegetables, scrubbed clean of every last trace of earth, lie securely within their germ-free packs, sealed as tightly as a hospital hypodermic. Bright red cuts of meat, trimmed, portioned and vacuum-packed, have nothing to indicate that they once formed part of a living animal. Salads are washed, bagged and ready to eat, guaranteed free of slugs, caterpillars and other refugees of the natural world. They might as easily have come from a high-tech factory on an industrial park.

And these are just the 'fresh' foods. Most of the foods we eat at home have been mechanically or chemically altered in some way to separate them still further from the life of the countryside. They have been minced into burgers or cheesy lasagnes; grated, chopped and sprinkled on to pizzas; emulsified, hardened, tenderised, flavour-enhanced and extruded, so they are no longer the 'whole' foods of the land. They are now ready-prepared, microwave-friendly tasty snack foods and instant TV dinners.

Most of their ingredients will have come from the land somewhere. But in the final product the original identities of those ingredients will be scarcely recognisable. They may have been sourced almost anywhere in the world – from a broiler shed in Taiwan to a hog-fattening factory in Ohio. If they are from the British countryside there is nothing to show it. And this is exactly what their makers intended.

For the manufacturers who produce the bulk of our food and the retailers who sell it there is every reason to disguise its true farm origins from the final consumer. Company profits rest on their ability to turn natural foods into manufactured brands. That is the purpose of all the washing and trimming, the processing and packaging. It is to transform the real foods of the countryside into products that can carry the company name. In this way the consumer's allegiance is lost to the grower and secured by the processor. Real foods are the gift of farmers and the land; products are the gift of corporations.

And so we come to believe that our lives are sustained by the activities not of farmers, but of Unilever, Kellogg's and McDonald's. We are convinced that without ten thousand juggernaut lorries thundering up and down the motorways every day of the year we will quickly starve. Yet wherever we live on this small island we are close to deep, rich soil that might be feeding us far better if it were not suffering from our neglect or continuous abuse by the techniques of industrial agriculture.

By distorting our perceptions of food the manufacturers and multiple retailers have succeeded in creating a dependency culture among a largely urban population, thus securing for themselves the lion's share of the billions we spend on food and driving down returns to farmers. We can hardly blame them for this. It is the way all large corporations behave under free-market capitalism. We might as well complain that a handful of large companies have succeeded in tying up the markets for small cars or feature films or computer software.

Like the commodity producers of the Third World, British farmers are now powerless to influence their customers. Their markets are under the control of strong corporations. Farmers and growers must produce to the specifications laid down by those corporations and accept whatever pared-down prices they are offered. It is a harsh regime under which only the most efficient farmers will survive. The new lords of food retailing seem virtually impregnable. Yet they wield their immense power only because farmers have allowed them to do it.

In provincial France things are a little different. Here good food is still associated with the land and the countryside in the minds of a large section of the population, even those in towns. Consumers still flock to the thriving street markets for the fresh and locally processed foods of the region. Supermarkets continue to stock local products and are not solely dependent on foods trucked in from some distant depot. French consumers value the fruits of the countryside and respect the farmer as their provider, while we in Britain distrust farmers and put our faith in the brand name on the box. It is surely no coincidence that the strongest opposition to the onward march of 'McDonald's culture' through Europe has arisen in France. In Britain the local McDonald's is the busiest restaurant in town.

CUTTING THE LINK WITH THE LAND

For the mass of Britons the link with the land was severed with the advance of industrialisation and the manufacturing towns during the nineteenth century. A growing urban population no longer linked food to the farms and fields around them. In the space of a generation or two they had lost contact with the land. The first to benefit from this rural alienation were the farmers and ranchers on the vast virgin territories of the United States and of British dominions around the world. They found a ready market for their meat and wheat among city dwellers who felt no particular loyalty to the produce of their own countryside.

Then came the major food manufacturers, moving in to exploit the growing confusion of an urban population about the nature of real food. The manufacturers offered their own mythology to replace the old certainties of people in close contact with the soil. Little by little they built up the dependency culture that would secure their customer base across the generations. And for three-quarters of a century government policies on agriculture helped them in their bid to establish a stranglehold on the nation's diet.

THE EFFECT OF SUBSIDIES SINCE THE 1930s

From the ending of the protective Corn Laws in 1846 Britain pursued a free-trade policy which lasted until the early 1930s. During this period – the First World War excepted – agriculture had no more claim to state financial support than any other of the great industries. Farming was expected to stand on its own feet in competition with farmers around the world.

Then in 1931, following a decade of agricultural depression, Britain finally abandoned free trade and began to introduce a measure of protection for the main farm products. Protection for farmers was consolidated in the great 1947 Agriculture Act which introduced comprehensive subsidies for a wide range of farm commodities. Since then agricultural production has enjoyed an unprecedented measure of state support, first from the national exchequer and then, in the final quarter of the twentieth century, from the EU.

Subsidies greatly increased the dependence of consumers on highly processed foods, by enabling food manufacturers to buy in their raw materials at world prices. At the time of the BSE crisis of the 1990s, manufacturers at the economy end of the burger market were budgeting just 20p per kg for their meat, a target they met by making full use of mechanically recovered scraps.

By choosing such products consumers hand over control of their diets – and ultimately of their health – to food technologists and finance directors of manufacturing companies. Britain's consumers currently spend around £60 billion on food, of which less than 20% ends up with the farmer. The rest goes to the companies who process it, package it and haul it from one end of the country to the other, or to the multiple retailers who sell it. This, more than anything, is why the countryside is in crisis. It is because we urban consumers have been persuaded to spend our food budgets with a handful of big manufacturing corporations instead of with the farmers who grow it.

Each year the wasteful CAP dispenses a little over £3 billion to British farmers, locking them into environmentally damaging methods of husbandry to produce cut-price raw materials for food companies. Real markets offering good profits, like those for many organic foods, are ignored. They must be met by imported supplies. Shackled by the EU inducements, British farmers go on farming for the subsidies, producing bog-standard commodity products, many of which are in surplus around the world, and in any case can be produced more cheaply elsewhere.

For this meagre offering farmers compliantly hand over the real rewards of their activities to manufacturing industry. And the nation suffers as a result. Consumers are denied a decent diet and are open to exploitation by the food industry. Farmers are denied a fair reward for their work and are driven ever deeper into despair. It is a national malaise, a chronic and largely unrecognised condition that drains resources, saps public health and destroys the spirit of the nation. And it could so easily be remedied.

The instinctive reaction of many farmers faced with falling returns is simply to produce more. When the milk price began a steep slide in the late 1990s a number of dairy farmers reacted by borrowing more money to increase the size of their herds and expand the facilities they needed to house them. The rationale – underpinned by farm business consultants – is that by increasing output it is possible to spread such overheads as land charges across a greater volume of production and so reduce unit production costs.

It is the classic, knee-jerk response of farmers encountering hard times. But far from helping it has pushed many even deeper into the mire. They are saddled with bigger debts that must be serviced from a falling income. A better response might have been to seek advice on how to market the product better and so increase returns from the existing output – by converting to organic production, for example, or by joining with others to establish a cooperative processing facility.

SHADOWS OF THE PAST

Marketing is something most farmers don't think they are any good at, so most don't bother with it. They look instead to expand output. It is a habit formed in the far-off post-war days when Europe was short of food and there was a ready market for almost anything farmers chose to produce. But the mindset is of little help in charting a course through global markets awash with food.

At the start of the twenty-first century farmers are still driven by a powerful piece of mythology that dates back to the nineteenth. It concerns the catastrophe that accompanied the last great experiment in a free-market food system. It is still cited as a dire warning of what could happen when the European tariff barriers are finally dismantled, opening up the UK to a fresh influx of cheap food imports from America, the Far East and Australasia.

To this day farmers repeat the grim tales learned at a parent's knee of capital values halved and tenant farms abandoned; of weed-choked crops and blocked field drains; of despair, decay and dereliction. Such are the inevitable consequences of a *laissez-faire*, free trade in agricultural goods, they warn. A new global market would unleash the selfsame forces of rural devastation.

Though there is truth in such tales, it is far from the whole truth. Those farmers hardest hit by the late nineteenth century depression were the farmers of eastern England, the region of crops and beef cattle principally. This was the fiefdom of the large arable farmer, heavily mechanised even a century ago, and reliant on employed rather than family labour. When the grain price collapsed under the weight of foreign imports they still had the wage bills to pay.

In western areas farms were smaller and mostly family-run. As now, they were predominantly in the business of stock-raising, beef-fattening, dairy farming and making farmhouse butter and cheese. For almost half a century after the ending of the Corn Laws these products remained relatively free of foreign competition. When the refrigerated ships began bringing in beef from the New World, the impact on prices was far less severe than for grain. The UK population was growing fast, and in the expanding manufacturing cities working people had more money to spend on food. Consequently the demand for meat remained firm.

While it is true that subsequent imports of factory cheese and butter took their toll on home-produced farmhouse products, it was those of poor quality that were most severely affected. Good-quality farm cheeses and butter continued to find profitable domestic markets. Imports had the effect of making bad farmhouse products – of which there were many in Victorian Britain – virtually unsaleable. As often happens, imports raised quality standards.

British agriculture responded to the fresh breezes of foreign competition by reducing its reliance on arable cropping and switching to a pastoral economy. Everywhere wheat land was ploughed and sown down to grass. In Essex, for example, the area under permanent grassland rose by 40% in the last two decades of the nineteenth century, while the area under wheat fell by 30%. In Essex, as in parts of East Anglia, bankrupt arable farms were taken over by livestock farmers migrating from the West Country, the Midlands and Scotland to set up dairy farms for supplying milk to the capital.

With the development of railways and the introduction of pasteurisation, farmers at a distance from the major cities were able to switch to fresh milk production and transport it swiftly to meet an expanding urban market. Though the bottom might have fallen out of the corn business, British agriculture had a new 'sheet anchor' – dairy farming. A time of deep recession gave birth to an enterprise that was to dominate the industry for a century.

While the free market may have spelled disaster for many specialist arable growers, it created new opportunities for livestock farmers, especially those making the effort to market high-quality products. Today the EU support system has enticed thousands of farmers into specialist crop production, the farming system most vulnerable to fluctuations in global commodity prices. But for the family farmers of the West – most of whom remain in livestock production – a freeing-up of food trading may not be the unmitigated disaster that they fear. On the contrary, it may yet presage a new 'golden age' for British farming, if it can take advantage of the new demands opened up by increasingly diffused affluence.

MARKETING FRESH FOOD FROM TODAY'S FARMS

Farmers complain that when shoppers step into the supermarket they instinctively search out the cheapest. But few farmers have seriously tested the assumption. Rarely have they attempted to brand their products, to add value by changing the perception of their lamb, beef, milk or vegetables in the way that food manufacturers do. Try telling the global food corporations that there are no profits to be made on food because consumers aren't prepared to spend real money on it. They'll have a ready reply. Produce the right product and attach it to a compelling brand image and it'll sell for a good price.

Farmers start with a clear advantage over the food companies. Almost by definition their products are better. The fresh, naturally produced foods of the countryside are almost always superior to the highly processed product. But until now farmers have squandered this intrinsic value by sending them off to the local creamery or market without any thought for how they might be marketed better. Even quality products get lumped in with the rest. As a result they pick up the 'sink' price set by global surpluses swilling around commodity markets.

It is a culture created and reinforced by more than half a century of state subsidy. Yet if farmers fail to value their own products sufficiently to market them properly, why should they expect their customers to pay a premium price, even though the foodstuff may warrant it? Cheap food policies have devalued the product. They have created the perception that foods of all sorts are worthless.

THE ORGANIC BRAND

Those farmers who have tried to brand their products have mostly met with success. The supreme example is the 'organic brand', the Soil Association symbol. Whatever the merits of organic food, few would deny its success in the market place. The organic experience provides a classic example of how value-added can transform the economic fortunes of agriculture.

Organic food now commands a substantial premium in the market place. In large part this is the result of information disseminated by a consistently positive press. There is every reason to expect the market to go on growing strongly. Organic farmers have made the reassuring discovery that the more people learn about food and farming, the more discriminating they become in the products they buy. This is a crucial observation for all farmers. It marks the clear route ahead for the whole of British agriculture.

Many farmers dismiss organic sales as a niche market, arguing that it will eventually reach saturation, at which point the premium will disappear. But on a small, heavily populated island like Britain, almost the entire output of the country's agriculture might be sold as a niche product. Why not Hereford beef raised on lush Worcester river meadows, or downland lamb reared on the flower-rich chalk grassland of the South Downs? Why not a Welsh cheese made from the milk of summer pastures high on the Cambrian Mountains? Why not link the values of a diverse, beautiful, much-loved landscape to the very products that flow from it?

TRANSFORMING BRITAIN'S FOOD CULTURE
The Farmer's Role

There will always be a market for 'commodity products', of course – the nomadic Cheddar from almost everywhere but Somerset, cheap beef for the low-cost burger market, basic quality wheat. But on an overpopulated island like Britain it makes little sense to produce for these markets. Better to leave that to the truly low-cost producers overseas, and concentrate on high-quality, premium products. British farmers can never be the world's cheapest producers, but they can aspire to be the best.

The branding of fresh British produce is no cynical exercise aimed at maximising profits. It is in the interests of the entire population. Urban consumers desperately need to be better informed about food. The messages they currently receive from the food industry are partial or distorted. When politicians and NGOs attempt to address this dangerous knowledge deficit they invite the taunt of 'nanny state', usually from those with some commercial interest in keeping the population in its present state of ignorance.

No one has a better reason than farmers for passing on the facts about food and the countryside. Changing the food culture of Britain will transform the fortunes of agriculture in the way that nothing else can. As organic farmers have discovered, the more consumers understand about food and farming the more they will seek out quality. And the more they will be prepared to pay for it.

The challenge for farmers is to accept responsibility for the nutritional quality and safety of the foods they produce. When the BSE crisis erupted, burger manufacturers were quick to switch to sources of supply outside Britain. They were bound to do this. They had their brands to protect. When customers buy a product the manufacturer accepts responsibility for their safety and welfare in relation to that product. Had farmers adopted the same approach to the 'fresh British food brand' in the mid-1980s they would have been marching on Whitehall demanding more effective action against the new cattle disease instead of playing their part in keeping it from the public gaze.

The 'Assured British Food' label, now appearing on supermarket foods across the country, is at least a start in the process of branding the products of the countryside. But there is a long way to go. Instead of mounting rearguard actions against every proposed improvement in animal welfare or environmental quality, farmers need to turn themselves into champions for a humane and ecologically healthy countryside. These are potent brand images for their products. How can a food be seen as healthy, life-enhancing and worthy of a decent price when it comes from a farmland landscape in which bird populations have been in free fall since the 1960s?

Farmers still think of themselves as victims. They feel let down because the state will no longer offer the promises and guarantees it made in the 1940s, when a hungry nation was grateful for whatever food it could get and no one worried too much about the wildflowers in the meadow. Now people want the best food they can get plus the wildflowers as well. This is not a disaster for agriculture. It is a rock-solid assurance that there are good times ahead for those farmers with the initiative to get into the market place and explain the facts about the countryside and how it works. Farmers can become national heroes again if they will but seize the opportunity.

The Politician's Role

There is much the government can do to ease this cultural transformation. A renewed attack on the discredited CAP ought to get a high priority. It remains a national scandal that after countless attempts at reform the policy continues to pour public money into the production of unwanted crops by methods that damage the environment. The money released by real reform would be far better used in the reconstruction of agriculture to serve the countryside.

Some of the money could be redirected into countryside management schemes for restoring some of the countless acres of wildlife habitat destroyed during decades of industrial farming. There could be help for farmer groups setting up regional cooperatives to market branded farm foods, while more funds could be found to encourage organic farming and other sustainable forms of agriculture. The government might also look into ways of opening up the on-line marketing of food. The Internet offers farmers a way of making direct contact with consumers, bypassing the supermarkets with their stranglehold on food retailing.

Most important of all the politicians might start looking for ways to remedy the alarming ignorance of food and farming by the population at large and by young people in particular. The omission from the National Curriculum of any comprehensive treatment of food, nutrition and cooking is nothing less than a betrayal, as a new generation is left prey to the blandishments of the food manufacturing industry.

HEALING THE TOWN–COUNTRY SCHISM

At its heart the crisis in rural Britain stems from the great divorce between town and country. Enclosures and two centuries of industrialisation have produced parallel cultures on one small, crowded island; a national schizophrenia from which all have suffered. It is only the healing of this schism that will bring about the true renaissance of agriculture. Those who present the town as the enemy of the countryside are no friends of farmers. Urban dwellers hold the key to the renewal of British agriculture. The challenge is to help them understand.

A HEALTHY FUTURE FOR FARMING

Hugh Oliver-Bellasis

'YOU CAN HAVE agriculture without the countryside but you cannot have countryside without farming.' (John Green)

At a time when the agricultural industry finds itself in deep crisis, nobody in authority appears to understand or care about the consequences, let alone try to find a solution.

A new farming strategy is long overdue. It must determine which areas are no longer suitable for commodity production, which warrant support for their wildlife value, and which should be developed.

IS FOOD PRODUCTION IMPORTANT?
European and UK attitudes

The European attitude is founded on a fragile food supply due to war. During those wars, many of the European countries were occupied and starved. Thus agricultural policy became the cornerstone of the original Common Market.

After the last war, the UK's infrastructure remained intact, whilst the EU countries' infrastructure had been destroyed. The UK was never occupied and that has profoundly affected agricultural policymaking. The CAP emerged as a direct result of concern about food supplies and threat of war from Russia.

These various pressures cause European governments to have different attitudes to farming. The political pressures arising from many factors, not least the size of the farming vote, skew the debate and ensure that change happens slowly.

European farmers are clearly trying to compete in a world market, but cannot produce commodities as cheaply as other parts of the world. But the administrators and many farmers do not recognise the facts. Sugar is a good example.

Agriculture has been supported in all industrialised developed countries in one way or another for many years. The disadvantage of support systems is that they remove the producer from the reality of the market. The antagonism voiced in the Uruguay round of GATT was aimed not only at our support system, but also at the disposal of surplus.

The Common Agricultural Policy

So why is the CAP failing? It achieved its original aims, but today those policies have become outdated because of globalisation. The failure has been in not adapting to change as world food markets matured. The politicians and the farming industry itself have appeared not to realise that these evolving markets demand radical change. Occasional short-ages and the immensely strong trade associations protected the industry from itself. Reforms have consistently under-performed. Can one policy ever work across the EU, and is it even realistic to strive to deliver 'a new CAP'?

The UK Context

Is the UK really different? Our farmers are broadly similar in attitude and equal in skill to their mainland counterparts. Farmers work on an open industrial estate. The taxpayer has a large stake in the industry and yet farming is made up of thousands of individuals, many of who own their own land and run small private businesses. Since the war, those individual businesses have been led by the policy reins of government, and latterly the EU, to a point where farmers no longer control their own business. But the government has not accepted that it is responsible for this plight. Consumer attitudes affect regulatory control, which then influences pro-duction. But the regulators' attitude to their exercise of that control in part is driven by fear of individual accountability in the event of a mistake. BSE is a sad example.

The rest of the EU is some way behind – and other countries in the world have not even thought about changing. Regulatory and other costs swallow up a progressively larger percentage of production costs as prices fall. The downward price pressure is further increased by the buying power of retailers and multi-nationals. There is no sector within the UK agricultural industry, nor any in the EU, that makes a sufficient return to reinvest in their businesses, almost irrespective of structure or land quality. Despite their protestations, the processors and retailers buy on price alone. The old adage used of retailers holds true: 'If the price is right forget the standards'. In any case, imported meat is not identifiable after carcasses are 'broken down'.

The Countryside – A Workplace?

The EU states treat their countryside in a variety of ways and the laws of land ownership differ. More importantly the scale of the public's interest is different. The countryside remains the farmers' industrial base, their workplace, and it is 'multi-functional'. In the UK, we have a small, densely populated island. Our population is the same as that of France, but squeezed into half the area. Should the financial support received by our farmers include provision for the countryside? The public's requirement from the countryside is not always easily balanced with current production. If our processors and retailers cannot purchase UK products at a price that enables our farmers to trade profitably, where does that place UK production? The key question is: 'Does HMG wish farmers to produce food in the UK and so protect the productive capability of the land?' If not, how do we protect that land's productive capability and meet biodiversity targets without growing a crop?

Support Systems

Most of the current support systems are out-of-date. Farmers have altered crop rotations to maximise the support they receive, rather than optimising returns from the crop grown. The recent reforms widened the gap between most farmers and the market place for their product. Government must shoulder some blame. But other players must be culpable, particularly trade associations. There has been a tendency to consider only the mechanisms by which the money is applied, rather than to find a policy that helps the industry to prosper. Admittedly those organisations have had their hands full dealing with the plethora of rules, regulations and laws emanating from Brussels and being implemented in the UK. But they have had the opportunity to change the outcome and they still have.

First, trade organisations have to be courageous and tell their members what has been happening. They must explain the harsh reality of the global trading. They must think through new strategies. They must highlight the need for a countryside dimension in policy and stop pretending that UK farmers are competitive. They must help to enable production and processing synergy that will benefit everyone. They must publicly articulate the secrecy that surrounds the retailers, their processors and production standards. Are the UK's organic standards comparable to the 75% of product imported?

The negotiators have been dealing with day to day issues, while putting strategy in the 'Too Difficult' tray. Certainly the Government seems unwilling to consider policies that take into account the long production cycles of agriculture. A satisfactory outcome to day-to-day issues only saves today's cost rather than adding profit. What is clear is that the recent leadership has been poor, preferring to appease rather than lead.

There is no escape from the sad fact that ministers have outmanoeuvred farming leaders. They have led those leaders to decisions and actions which they knew to be beneficial to government, though undoubtedly damaging to the industry. Sadly, the ministers do not seem to care. They do not understand the countryside, and are happy to actively disadvantage it, while professing to listen to its problems.

In addition the farming industry and its leaders have failed to recognise the power and value of teamwork. They failed to harness the support of other organisations, small or large, from Livestock Marketing Alliance to RSPB, because they find their public criticisms uncomfortable. They merely belittle their contribution, instead of working with them. This must change and change fast; time is short. Maybe they should be reminded that 'a sign of greatness is taking advice'.

Trading Influences

The EU cannot ignore the rest of the world. The 'Freedom to Farm' policy in America was a masterstroke. It allowed the President to 'support' farmers legitimately. Payments in excess of $13 billion over two years were deemed not to be 'trade-distorting' under WTO rules. It also allowed the US to regain export markets. In contrast the CAP is trade-distorting, leaving Europe open to international criticism. Both the failure of CAP reform in Berlin, through national interest, and the failure of the Seattle round of the WTO have increased the need for a different approach.

The picture is further complicated by globalisation, which is illustrated by the continuing aggregation of businesses in every sector across the world. This puts price pressure on manufacturing businesses. Costs are passed down the chain, until they can go no further – to the primary producer.

Products can now be purchased from anywhere in the world and be with the purchaser within twenty-four hours. This applies equally to dry or perishable goods, thanks to modern technology. Production is carried out under very varied regulatory conditions and with work forces who have completely different expectations – no minimum wage laws for the Pacific Rim; no commitment to pensions for Brazilian cattlemen. Yet HMG and some trade associations continue to pretend that the UK farmer can compete with the best in the world in any discipline.

Further East: The CEE States

There is huge pressure to integrate the Central and Eastern European states (CEE) into the EU to provide political stability. While the CAP becomes increasingly discredited, those states long to join the EU, coveting its support systems and encouraged by words from EU leaders, who disregard the cost. But those levels of support will never be economic. The CEE has the residue of communism to wash away. Their agricultural systems are probably twenty-five years behind the EU, despite having excellent climate and soils. Their general standards – of animal welfare, disease control, pollution control, water management, hygiene standards, health and safety regulations – differ from those in force in EU states. This does not mean that there is necessarily consequent danger, although there may be a higher risk, which CEE consumers are happy to accept, since the alternative is starvation.

We must debate the cost to production systems of pollution to water supplies, high welfare systems and wildlife management, probably on a WTO basis, but certainly within the EU. If we do not, the damage of the last 40 years will be repeated in the remainder of Europe. That damage is already evident in some places.

When will politicians and civil servants realise the impact of their policies on natural systems? Government agencies are not keen to spend money on monitoring. Equally, monitoring is the only way to test whether agricultural policy is delivering solutions. Because wildlife is dependent on management of species or vegetation, farming policy is critical.

Reform

Therefore the only conclusion is real reform. Centuries ago, Socrates said, 'He who aspires to statesmanship must first understand wheat'. Do we need to produce that food in the EU or import cheaper product from around the world? If we produce food, we must evaluate the cost of society's constraints on the production system. How will the land be used if food is not produced? Will it return to scrub?

I believe we must continue to manage the land. We need an integrated policy that will deliver viable farming within a wider countryside. Sadly, our trade associations and many of their members refuse to debate the long-term needs of farming. They devote little resource to original thought.

CAP – Where Next?

Reform of the CAP will be an acid test of EU thinking. Any federalist moves will be emasculated if there continues to be no effective policy for food production within the countryside. The European Agricultural Trade Association (COPA) must start to lead. There is no sign that the national governments have any intention of true reform. This situation is as lamentable as it is dishonest.

The starting-point is for farmers and their associations across the EU to admit the necessity for radical reform. They must recognise the difficulties, then agree that national or regional interest has to be put to one side, in order to enable a cross-European countryside policy to be developed. That process must be inclusive of countryside interests and it must encompass all parts of the food chain. It must include the CEE states which hope to join the EU.

In Europe, there is a need to identify what crops are best suited to a particular region, so that natural advantage is maximised. Any support must be synchronised with the WTO rules. Thus specific crops, animals or products will no longer be supported. Will the tobacco regime disappear or the sugar regime be altered?

There is a need to realign thinking in DGvi, so that they recognise and take into account major conservation problems. A good example is Spain: the loss of a number of bird species is due to alterations to its agricultural systems encouraged by CAP support.

Critically, there is little obvious dialogue between the Directorates which influence the countryside. People say: 'We cannot do anything until the CAP is reformed'. But the CAP will never be reformed so long as national interest takes precedence. Politicians need to hear the alarm call: there is crisis and they are in the hot seat. If an integrated policy was seen to be taking shape, the other members of WTO might debate farming and countryside matters with the EU. Fewer people will make a living from agriculture, though maybe similar numbers will be employed in the countryside. There will come a time when biotechnology allows a variety of crops to be grown for pharmaceutical purposes. Perhaps the land will become a natural laboratory. However, in the UK that will take longer, since the GM issue has so far been seriously mishandled.

Sadly, if attitudes persist in the Council of Agriculture Ministers, it is possible that farm policy would be nationalised, which might disadvantage the UK. Our government's commitment over the years does not compare favourably with the other member states. The rural vote does not attract Ministers' attention; it is too small, hence the frustration evident in rural areas.

However, there are things the industry can do for itself: the key is the combination of adding value through traceability and quality, combined with an interest in the processing chain. This challenge is Mount Everest twice in one day, but we do have the courage, ability and the ingenuity.

Finally

Farmers have no right to a market. Each has to manage the individual farm as a player in the countryside team. The links further along the chain – transport, merchant, abattoir, mill, malting, processor, and manufacturer – are also involved. How can we start a process of combined change?

First, the government must state that it will protect the productive capability of the land as a national asset. Immediately, the industry will have the confidence to build the necessary links in this fragile chain and will cease to feel abandoned. The government in partnership with farmers and processors must then set out a framework in which integrated food businesses can emerge with no support, but with incentives. These might include matters of tax or planning or any measure that reduces set-up costs and encourages invest-ment, but is not trade distorting. These new enterprises would have to demonstrate clear partnerships in the chain.

The harsh reality is that, without action of this kind, there will be no future for farming of any consequence in the United Kingdom.

A strategic policy group (Royal Commission) must be

formed by EU governments, including the CEE countries, to bring together the food chain, farming groups, countryside groups, allied industries, together with food experts. They must draw up a completely new agricultural policy, which determines which areas are non-competitive for agriculture and identifies whether those areas have a wildlife potential, which warrant support. If so, what management is necessary and who will do it? The products of this new agricultural system must be fashioned by market forces. An outline plan should be taken to the WTO, as a blueprint for their next round of talks for all other trading blocs to follow suit.

If this sort of initiative is not started shortly, not only will there be a continuing descent into disaster, but also real battle will break out at the WTO table. We shall only have ourselves to blame – and the losers will be the people and the countryside.

Foot-and-Mouth Disease: An Evaluation of the Current Control Policy From a Historical Perspective

Abigail Woods

HISTORY IS COMMONLY used as a resource by MAFF to justify the policy of foot-and-mouth disease (FMD) control by slaughter. The adherence to the same policy for 100 years and its supposed ongoing efficacy provide considerable authority for its continual application, despite the fact that at present, the disease situation is worsening daily.

If the time has arrived to examine whether slaughter should continue, then these historical certainties also require questioning. The past not only offers guidance where similar situations appear in the present, but also reveals profound differences which suggest that direct parallels cannot always be drawn between past and present.

Two years' research using original documents have contributed to the following comments:

1) Slaughter has never been the obvious response to FMD. Complex, ongoing negotiations were necessary in order to gain support for the introduction and maintenance of government control over FMD. The rationale behind this

decision was largely tied to the economic, commercial and agricultural conditions of the nineteenth century. It cannot therefore be simply assumed that this past decision still holds, as at the very least its rationale must have changed to keep pace with the changing understanding of FMD and alterations in agriculture and world trade patterns.

2) The fact that slaughter has always eliminated FMD has contributed to the present authority of this policy. However, on several occasions stamping out has taken months if not years, with profound personal and economic costs which are not generally publicised. On such occasions, slaughter has generated controversy, and I explain who was responsible for these criticisms, and why. I also present the likelihood that many problems experienced in the past will resurface as major issues affecting the outcome of the current crisis. Past evidence reveals that the present outbreak was always likely to reach this scale. This data forms a strong argument for reconsidering the proposed intensification of slaughter.

3) The authority of slaughter is such that MAFF firmly believes that there is no other way to manage FMD, especially given the technical and administrative problems with vaccines. Here I examine why MAFF is mistaken in this certainty which is largely grounded in past successes, and explore deeper reasons why vaccination is not favoured.

1) SLAUGHTER HAS NEVER BEEN THE OBVIOUS RESPONSE TO FMD[1]

a) state control of FMD

• FMD first appeared in 1839 yet despite initial reaction was largely ignored for the next 30 years. The disease was

[1] The majority of this section is drawn from my MSc thesis: A. Woods, 'From occupational hazard to animal plague: Foot-and-mouth disease in Britain, 1839–1884' Manchester University, 1999

common, extremely mild in relation to other prevalent diseases and provoked few efforts at control. FMD was an accepted and indeed expected occupational hazard.

- Many veterinarians, farmers and MPs rejected the need to control FMD, upon the basis that firstly the disease was not severe enough and that losses due to legislative 'cure' would outweigh those inflicted by the disease itself. Secondly they doubted if control were possible, given their belief that FMD could spread through wildlife and human movements, which could not be controlled as easily as infected livestock.

- Influential breeders, often MPs and Royal Agricultural Society representatives, led the lobby for FMD elimination. They suffered the most marked economic losses due to the disease: valuable young livestock suffered higher than average mortality while infertility, occasional abortions and mastitis were also recognised to follow FMD infection.

- Quantification of FMD losses was an important resource in the drive for FMD elimination. Various farming witnesses to Parliamentary Commissions put forward their empirical estimates of financial losses caused by the disease. These were expressed in terms of extra feed consumed, reduction in milk production or extra time required to make market weight. In 1871 the disease was made notifiable, and by multiplying disease incidence by these estimates it became possible to express FMD losses on a national scale for the first time. These contributed to the desire to eliminate the disease because it seemed obvious that FMD affected the meat supply, and meat consumption by the working classes was believed necessary in order to increase their working efficiency. This stimulated urban, capitalist demands for FMD control.

- Successful efforts to intensify FMD controls failed to reduce disease spread. This meant that many farmers experienced movement and marketing restrictions which in their minds became inseparably linked to FMD occurrence. The social and economic effects of such measures meant that farmers began to dread FMD and demand its elimination. By the 1880s therefore, the battle over whether FMD should be subject to state-led control was won and the framework for today's FMD controls were in place. Imports of livestock from FMD infected countries were prohibited (most European nations sending livestock to Britain had FMD), disease spread was halted by isolation of infected and contact animals, markets were cancelled and movement restrictions imposed within large infected areas. Whether these measures worked or the disease disappeared for other reasons is difficult to assess, but Britain was remarkably free of FMD from 1884–1900.

To conclude:

Therefore the original desire to eliminate FMD was facilitated by the following factors:

- State controls of other contagious diseases were necessary and therefore the framework for FMD regulation existed.
- Breeders perceiving FMD as a disease inflicting severe economic losses upon their valuable stock possessed the political power to impress these notions upon others.
- The capitalist fear that reduction in the meat supply by FMD would spark civil unrest and reduce workers' productivity levels.
- Most other farmers eventually reconstructed FMD as a severe disease despite the mild nature of its symptoms, because of the implications of measures undertaken by the state for its control.
- It is obvious therefore that the decision to control FMD occurred within a society very different to the present, especially in terms of where the political power lay and in the beliefs about the value of meat consumption.

b) State slaughter for FMD

- Official histories state that slaughter was first introduced in 1884. This requires qualification; while an act was passed in 1884 enabling local authorities to apply slaughter if they wished, this was only implemented once in the next 20 years.

- Slaughter was actually introduced 'by the back door' at a time when disease incidence was low, upon the basis that this would most rapidly eliminate disease before it had chance to spread. The imposition of British import controls in the 1880s encouraged many other FMD free nations such as the US and Australia to follow suit. This affected the British export trade, which almost solely consisted of British pedigree cattle owned by the same set of influential breeders. This small trade was nonetheless extremely valuable and therefore the need to keep the country clear of FMD was repeatedly asserted by breeders. However, when disease struck these pedigree herds were exempted of slaughter.

- The Ministry stated that they were too valuable to the nation to merit destruction though an additional motive was the huge compensation costs demanded by slaughter.[2] The Ministry persuaded the majority of farmers who were not involved in the export trade that slaughter was vital by portraying FMD as a disease which would inflict severe economic losses were it allowed to run. This fact was subject to repetition throughout the twentieth century as FMD continued to appear.[3] The nineteenth century estimates of losses inflicted by FMD were used as evidence, as were high loss estimates from the continent, where FMD was endemic. These figures were contrasted to low average annual costs to MAFF of

[2] CVO evidence to the 1922 Pretyman Committee, see Public Records Office (PRO) files MAF 35/159

[3] See *The Times'* references to FMD, 1920–1970 (sourced using *Palmer's Index to the Times*)

103

disease elimination by slaughter.[4] However, such statistics are extremely questionable. The method of loss estimation on the continent was never described. In addition, costs cited by MAFF did not express the often-substantial, consequential losses inflicted by FMD upon farmers and meat traders. The nineteenth-century estimates were themselves extremely empirical and no controlled experiments have since been undertaken to properly quantify the reduction in productivity of an FMD recovered animal.

- The original rationale for discriminate slaughter during the period 1900–1920 was supposedly to rapidly eliminate new invasions of FMD, and this was largely successful; outbreaks were contained quickly and costs kept low.[5] However, in 1922 (as in the present case), disease spread through an infected market yet notification was delayed, by which time FMD was already widespread. This was an entirely new context for the application of slaughter and certainly not one which the original framers of the slaughter policy had foreseen or intended.

To conclude:

This evidence undermines the authority of the state policy for control of FMD by slaughter. This was not the 'obvious' response to this disease. Slaughter of FMD was introduced almost by default in order to rapidly eliminate new outbreaks, and again by default was extended to the control of already-raging epidemics. Pressure for the continuation of this policy was not driven by far-sighted, intelligent men but by an influential group who manipulated their political power in order to preserve their personal economic interests.

[4] An example may be found in PRO file MAF 35/167, Precis of CVO's evidence, Departmental Committee 1924. SS Memo B, 'Slaughter versus Isolation, a Comparison.'
[5] see Board of Agriculture, Annual Reports under the Diseases of Animals Acts, 1900, 1908, 1911–1921

It is important to realise that animal welfare arguments were never part of the discussions upon FMD control. The present argument that slaughter is justified upon welfare grounds is merely a device intended to make slaughter a 'politically acceptable' move. Emphasising its economic basis would simply have fuelled pre-existing criticisms against the validity of intensive farming systems. This welfare argument is now exposed as a fallacy, given the proposed slaughter of many healthy sheep, some of which have supposedly suffered the disease without drawing notice to themselves.

However, arguments about the effect of FMD upon the export trade have become more cogent over time, as since the Second World War, and especially under recent trade developments in the EU and WTO, exports of British meat and livestock products have dramatically increased. As such, the majority of the farming community now possesses the same interests originally held by the few pedigree livestock breeders. Meanwhile, trade barriers erected against nations infected by FMD have intensified. Therefore despite the still highly questionable long-term economic effects of allowing FMD to become endemic, this is simply not an option and in terms of international trade, the need to eliminate FMD is greater than ever before.

If FMD elimination is required on economic grounds, then the veracity of the current approach is based upon the fact that elimination of disease by slaughter costs less than the long-term loss of the export market. If this ceases to be the case, then the policy should be reviewed and alternatives explored. It may be, for example, that the huge costs involved in the intensified cull outweigh the costs of the longer export ban which would result from vaccination.

2) THE PAST 'SUCCESS' OF SLAUGHTER REQUIRES QUALIFICATION

- FMD outbreaks occurred repeatedly throughout the twentieth century, with rarely a disease free year until

1969. In many years there were very few outbreaks and slaughter effectively and rapidly eliminated disease.[6]

- On other occasions however, control was not so efficient and while FMD was eventually stamped out, many animals lost their lives and the costs were huge, both in terms of MAFF compensation, farmers' consequential losses and the overall psychological impact of slaughter. History reveals that opposition to the slaughter policy was most marked in these years. The 1922–24 outbreak effectively lasted 2 years, despite a few weeks of disease freedom in 1923. In 1951–52 disease elimination took almost a year,[7] and the 1967–68 outbreak lasted 8 months. While slaughter can be said to have 'worked', the Ministry generally overlooks the events of these years and dismisses the criticisms that emerged as unfounded and ignorant. In 1924, a severe revolt by Cheshire farmers meant that MAFF was forced to allow the isolation of several herds rather than slaughter.[8] In 1968, MAFF was on the verge of vaccination given the rapid spread of disease. Only the down-turn in notifications prevented this strategy going ahead.[9] Slaughter has therefore not always been as successful as MAFF claims.

- The argument that slaughter is a totally inappropriate means of controlling FMD has always been an extreme minority position. Certainly in the present, for the economic reasons stated above, few would dispute the fact that slaughter is a vital first line of defence against FMD.

- A more valid criticism is that slaughter, whilst in theory effective and the best means of controlling disease, is

[6] Anon, 'Foot and Mouth disease' in *Animal Health, a centenary, 1865–1965* (London, 1965)

[7] ibid, p279

[8] Information drawn from the *Cheshire Observer* and *Crewe Chronicle* newspapers, 12/23-2/24, located in Cheshire Public Records Office

[9] Personal communication, GRE Evans BVSc MRCVS

inappropriate to the control of widespread FMD. This point deserves consideration in the present situation. Arguments which have historic roots yet are applicable to the present include:

1) Ever since the introduction of this policy, MAFF has recognised that the rapid notification of disease is vital for its success. But this requires farmers to have a high index of suspicion that symptoms observed in their stock may be FMD. This is always a problem when FMD is absent for long periods and is compounded by the fact that symptoms are not always obvious. This fact has frequently stimulated intense efforts by the NFU and MAFF to 'educate' farmers of FMD symptoms.

2) Historically, the failure to rapidly detect FMD has led to diseased animals inadvertently infecting markets and transit vehicles, resulting in a sudden 'explosion' of FMD throughout the nation, presenting extreme tracing difficulties. The frequent movement of livestock through markets by dealers was recognised in 1922 as compounding this problem.[10]

3) The logistical problems presented by rapid spread of disease are well recognised from experiences in Cheshire in 1924 and 1967. Problems of manpower and supplies can prevent the rapid follow-up, diagnosis, slaughter and destruction of infected animals. These problems have been commonly cited by critics as permitting the ongoing spread of FMD and have also been recognised by government inquiries into FMD outbreaks. Animals are at their most infective while incubating disease, therefore if symptoms are present in only a few animals, their contacts are likely to be manufacturing large quantities of virus and if not slaughtered immediately pose a dangerous risk. Even once slaughtered, virus can survive in parts of the carcass, in buildings and be carried by wildlife. If

[10] FMD: Report of Pretyman Committee, Parliamentary Papers 1923, cmd 1794

disinfection and carcass disposal is not rapid and efficient, this poses additional routes for disease spread. When resources are extremely stretched, the Ministry has extreme difficulty overtaking and halting the spread of disease.[11]

4) When large-scale slaughter has occurred and yet disease is still spreading, opposition has frequently been directed to the sheer scale of the destruction. The Ministry tends to counteract this by stating that the percentage of livestock killed in national terms is extremely low. This is an attempt to disguise the fact that in certain regions, percentages are huge – 33% of Cheshire cattle in 1923–24[12] and 1967–68.[13] In these cases, farmers argued that disease controls had failed, and that elimination only occurred because there were no longer any livestock left to infect.[14] In addition, the psychological effects of large-scale slaughter become widespread and while not quantifiable are extremely pervasive.[15] Critics also assert the immorality of slaughtering huge numbers of animals (especially breeding stock not destined for the butcher in the near future) when alternative disease controls are available (see below).

[11] CVO evidence to the Pretyman Committee, 1924 (PRO file MAF 35/164, 35/165) and evidence to the Northumberland enquiry, ch. 8 and 9 in H. Hughes and J. Jones, *Plague on the Cheshire Plain* (London, 1969), R. Whitlock, *The Great Cattle Plague* (1969), p87–92

[12] Evidence from Cheshire local newspapers cited above

[13] R. Whitlock, *The Great Cattle Plague* (London, 1969), p58

[14] Evidence from Cheshire local newspapers cited above

[15] On both these cited occasions, the depressing effects of fires and smoke were cited as severely affecting morale. (CVO evidence to the 1924 Pretyman Committee, H. Hughes and J. Jones, *Plague on the Cheshire Plain* (1969). In 1923 Cheshire it was also widely believed (as has been cited in the present outbreak) that smoke from fires carried the virus. See letter from J. E. M. Sloane on cremation, *Crewe Chronicle* 22/12/23 p7

5) The cost of compensating for large-scale slaughter is huge. The Ministry has in the past attempted to overcome these criticisms by expressing compensation in terms of annual averages over a number of years. It also repeatedly states that the cost of slaughter is worthwhile given the economic losses inflicted by the stoppage of British exports.[16] A cost-benefit study undertaken as part of the enquiry into the 1967–68 epidemic is repeatedly cited as stating that slaughter was the cheapest and preferred method of disease control.[17] In fact the authors of this admitted to a number of major methodological problems encountered with this technique,[18] including the difficulty of quantifying factors such as the uncertainty and stress which the slaughter policy imposed upon farmers.[19]

- Historically, the NFU executive has always supported MAFF in the decision to slaughter. However, at grass roots levels there has been considerable dissent, but regional opinions are often discarded by headquarters.[20] The NFU supposedly represents many different branches of farming throughout the nation. Yet regional variations in farming practices and the fact that all branches of farming do not share the same interests means that the task of representing farmers as a whole is extremely difficult. Since the 1920s, the NFU has been recognised by MAFF as the foremost farming representative body and

[16] An example may be found in the Public Records Office, file MAF 35/167, Precis of CVO's Evidence, FMD Departmental Committee, 1924

[17] A. P. Power and S. Harris, 'A Cost-Benefit Evaluation of Alternative Control Policies for Foot-and-Mouth Disease in Great Britain.' *J Agri Econ* 24 (1973), 573-600

[18] ibid, p574

[19] ibid, p594

[20] Evidence for this may be found in the NFU minutes from meetings of the Meat and Livestock Committee, held at Reading Rural History Unit

has been involved in many complex negotiations in order to gain overall state benefits for the industry.[21] Small wonder therefore that the NFU does not wish to divorce itself from its benefactors in response to criticism arising from a proportion of farmers.

- The British Veterinary Association has always shown similar alliances, despite grass roots objections to slaughtering. Again however, one must bear its additional interests in mind. The veterinary profession has gained considerably in status over the years, not least as a result of state recognition as experts in the fields of research and public health. MAFF has been used as a vehicle in the past to expand the veterinary role and reward systems.[22]

- Members of the medical profession have historically been involved in major criticisms of the slaughter policy.[23] For obvious reasons, doctors tend to rely on therapy and vaccination for disease control and this reliance on scientific, laboratory-formulated measures has shaped criticisms of a supposedly backward and barbaric slaughter policy. However, medical criticisms have been repeatedly rejected by farmers and vets upon the basis that doctors are only experts in the field of human disease and have no role to play in the management of livestock

[21] The early problems faced by the NFU are described in G. Cox, P. Lowe and M. Winter, 'The Origins and Early Development of the NFU' Ag Hist Review 39 (1991), 30-47. An interesting analysis of unionism and the close relationships between union leaders and government may be found in H. Perkin, 'The Corporate State' in H. Perkin, The Rise of Professional Society. England since 1880 (London, 1990)

[22] This conclusion is drawn from extensive reading of the Veterinary Record from the 1920s onwards, and from several Parliamentary Committees appointed in the first half of the twentieth century to consider the present and future veterinary requirements.

[23] One of the most prominent critics in the 1920s was Walter Morley Fletcher, the first Secretary of the Medical Research Council. See PRO file FD 1/1346

problems. It is important not to overlook the fact that certainly prior to WWII, medics and vets were competing for 'territory' in terms of which profession should be responsible for meat/milk inspection and for research into animal diseases.[24]

To conclude:

- The above reveals that the present situation is not entirely new, though unprecedented in the scale of slaughter proposed. The history of past outbreaks reveals that initial delay in notification and infection of several markets by dealers have been vital factors permitting FMD to evade control by slaughter and leading to extremely widespread disease. This perhaps points to the fact that the present scale of this outbreak could have been predicted as these facts came to light.
- It also reveals that while criticisms against the principle of slaughter as an initial means of disease control have little justification, there are many objections, voiced historically but nonetheless relevant today, to the continuation of large-scale slaughter once the disease is widespread. Not least of these is the logistical problem of efficiently implementing the slaughter policy upon a large scale. Farms affected now by FMD are far larger than in 1967, therefore the system of slaughter and disposal will be more rapidly overwhelmed and the problems associated are therefore more pressing.
- Opposition to slaughter tends to be written out of history, precisely because the individuals concerned are not always the most prominent or influential. However I can guarantee that in situations such as the present, when FMD is widespread and slaughter of questionable efficacy, there has always been considerable opposition to its continuation. It is important to recognise that external interests will always influence the positions individuals

[24] *Veterinary Record* evidence.

adopt upon the slaughter policy. Farmers may wish to keep their animals, but is this any worse a motive than the desire for personal economic or professional gain?

3) WHY THE HISTORICAL AUTHORITY OF SLAUGHTER AND REJECTION OF VACCINATION ARE INAPPROPRIATE RESPONSES

Authority of slaughter

- Britain has always been intensely proud of her ability to abolish disease. Our island status has meant that several diseases, once eliminated by stamping out have been permanently kept out of the country e.g. cattle plague, sheep pox, rabies. This geographical 'difference' has been continually emphasised as reason why disease elimination is achievable in Britain but rather more difficult elsewhere, and has been used by MAFF to justify the rejection of preferred continental means of disease control in favour of a stamping out policy.[25] However, this 'island' status has been increasingly undermined by the expansion of free European and world trade and widespread tourism. This encourages the introduction of 'foreign' substances into Britain. Powers to restrict such moves are extremely limited and inspection as a means of control can never approach 100% efficacy. The confidence in British isolation and its implications for disease control measures is therefore less justified than in the past.

- In addition the conditions within the nation have undergone profound changes. Farm size and livestock holdings have vastly increased throughout the twentieth century whilst the number involved in agriculture has plummeted. Agri-business has forced smaller producers out of the market while economies of scale and meat marketing

[25] Drawn from references to *The Times* and MAFF answers to Parliamentary Questions, 1920s–1970

practices have encouraged the nationwide movement of livestock. Indeed, a critic of slaughter in the 1950s uses the very same reasoning to support a call for alternative disease control measures.[26] While cattle passports, the smaller number of individuals involved and IT advances should assist livestock tracing, these are counterbalanced by the sheer numbers of stock involved.

- Not only has the entire context for FMD control changed, but the disease itself has been 'reinterpreted' in the light of novel epidemiological findings. In the nineteenth century, inconvenient FMD controls were eventually accepted due to the widespread belief that simple prohibition of diseased imports would keep the disease out of Britain. Yet the disease still appeared – foreign hay and straw was banned in 1908 after an outbreak was linked to this source. The 1920s saw prohibition of continental meat imports and the imposition of stringent controls on the Argentine as meat was recognised as a vehicle of the virus. Swill boiling regulations were introduced at this time.[27] At the same time, human movement in 1922–24 was linked to disease spread between farms,[28] and research in the 1920s and 30s investigated the potential role of wildlife, including birds, in epidemiological spread of disease.[29] Yet still FMD kept appearing and spreading despite all these additional precautions, highlighting its extreme contagiousness and virtual impossibility in sealing off all routes of disease spread. The recognition in 1968 that air currents could carry the virus is the ultimate example of how resistant this virus is to man-made restrictions. If these complexities had been realised at first, it is

[26] W. D. Thomas in the *Daily Telegraph*, 25/3/52
[27] 'FMD' in Anon, *Animal Health, a Centenary* (1965)
[28] Report of the 1924 Pretyman Committee on FMD
[29] Discussed frequently in Foot-and-Mouth Research Committee Papers and minutes from Committee Meetings during this period, located in Pirbright archives and the PRO

doubtful that legislative efforts and slaughter would ever have been thought appropriate to FMD management.

- However, it is confidence borne out of past successes against FMD which is spurring MAF to persist in slaughter and to repeatedly reject alternative measures. This confidence is misplaced; FMD has indeed been eliminated in the past but the world has changed and the past is no guarantee of future success. Despite many additional disease controls, no amount of regulation can control air or wildlife spread of FMD and disinfection of people and vehicles is primitive and largely useless.[30] The changing conditions of agricultural and international trade during the last fifty years can only assist this virus in its spread around the globe.

Rejection of Vaccines

- The notion that Britain could eliminate FMD by slaughter meant that while publicly MAFF expressed hopes that a vaccine would emerge from Pirbright (the FMD research lab set up in 1924), in private the CVO stated that vaccines would find no application on British soil. However, he considered that any scientific advances in disease control could be useful in areas where the disease was endemic, such as South America and Europe, since this would reduce the possibility of disease importation into Britain from these regions.[31]
- The fact that FMD is such a contagious virus justified the restriction of research, at least on large animals, to workers employed at Pirbright under the FMD Research Committee, over which MAFF had a huge degree of

[30] Concluded by the 1969 Northumberland committee and reported in the recent press, week of 12/3/01

[31] CVO letter to W. Leishman, (Major General, Army Medical Services) 7/1/24, arguing against Leishman's recommendation for immediate institution of research into FMD in Britain. PRO file MAF 35/217

influence. This made it impossible for independent researchers to investigate the disease and formulate alternative measures for its control.[32]

- The Ministry's stance meant that there was no sense of urgency in the British hunt for a vaccine, and most initial progress took place on the continent, when since the 1920s, serum was used for treatment and prevention of disease.[33] Only when war contingency planning was undertaken in Britain in 1937 did the need to develop a vaccine become more pressing. This was partly because of the perceived threat of FMD use as a biological weapon and also because under wartime meat shortages, slaughter may become impossible.[34]

- In the early 1950s, vaccines were used in Europe (with varying success) to counteract a severe outbreak of FMD.[35] When the disease reached Britain in 1951, there was a clamour for vaccine use. All work hitherto was kept secret since the Ministry feared such pressure. In 1951 however, MAFF was forced to account for how it had spent 30 years of research and hundreds of thousands of pounds if it was not to assist British farmers against FMD. MAFF stated that while vaccines were under development, their use in Britain was inappropriate since many technical problems had yet to be solved. Vaccines were only used on the continent due to the 'inferior' disease status there, which meant that slaughter was not financially feasible. Technical problems were less of an issue on the continent, as vaccines there were used to reduce

---

[32] The FMD Research Committee minutes, 1924–39 reveal the repeated rejection of external requests to investigate FMD

[33] Skinner, FMD Research Committee, Committee Paper 411 (1939), FMDRC 'Passive immunisation against FMD with special reference to the use of convalescent blood, a review'

[34] PRO file MAF 35/231 FMD (Bacteriological Warfare) and MAF 250/126 FMD: preparation of serum for treatment of animals

[35] Some information on this is revealed in PRO file MAF 35/868, European Commission for the control of FMD

disease spread, without the overall aim of elimination as was the situation in Britain.[36]

- For the past 50 years, these same arguments have been used against vaccination: the problem of strain diversity, the huge costs of repeatedly vaccinating animals against the disease and the fact that inactivated virus used in the vaccine may retain an element of infectivity and induce 'masked' disease or a carrier state.[37] In addition, the 'stigmatisation' of vaccine use remains – only nations which are unable to control the disease resort to vaccination. The barriers erected against goods from vaccinating nations merely reinforce this stigma, which originated on British soil.

- While many advances have been made in vaccination, it is clear that to MAFF, these advances will never be sufficient. The Ministry keeps moving the goal posts, such that nothing short of no-risk, 100% protection will be regarded as sufficient. This could hardly be claimed of any vaccine in existence. While good progress has been made in tests to differentiate infected and vaccinated animals – tests that have important implications for the export trade and considerably strengthen the case for vaccination – MAFF rejects these as insufficiently advanced for field application. This latter argument is again a long standing one. No aspect of vaccine technology has, in MAFF's view, ever been sufficiently advanced for use in the field. There is a huge irony in this situation – that despite a culture of scientific discovery that involves the transfer of discoveries out of laboratory into the field, MAFF seems intent on keeping FMD vaccines within the lab and locking the door.

- Other nations, currently disease free, are far more open to

[36] see the collection of press and journal cuttings made by H. Skinner during the 1950 outbreak, held in the Pirbright laboratory archives
[37] see R Whitlock, *The Great Cattle Plague* (1969), p78–79 and F. Brown, 'FMD – one of the remaining great plagues' *Proc R Soc Lond.* B 229 (1986), 215–226. Also see recent MAFF comments to the press, Feb–March 2001

vaccination. Australian experts state that 'recent developments suggest that vaccination could become a more attractive option.'[38] Not all European nations were happy at the decision to stop vaccinating against FMD in the EU in 1991, in order to streamline disease control policies and lift trade barriers, as recent comments in the press suggest.[39] The EU strategy for emergency FMD vaccination suggests a number of criteria which should affect the decision to vaccinate; the British situation already fulfils many of these, such as rapid rise in outbreaks and widespread disease distribution. The suggested rationale for using vaccination – to prevent FMD spread – is clearly present in this case.[40]

- Several of the scientific arguments against vaccination are irrelevant to Britain's current position. An example is the matter of strains, since only one strain is involved in this case, for which sufficient stocks of vaccine exist. The matter of repeatedly vaccinating animals is also inappropriate in this case, since vaccines would only be required in the short term to control disease rather than to prevent its re-importation. In addition, the argument that there is insufficient manpower to vaccinate livestock is surely irrelevant since farmers are quite capable of vaccinating their own stock without veterinary assistance. MAFF would probably argue against this in the name of absolute vaccine security but this argument has no real weight, it simply reflects the overall desire not to vaccinate.

[38] M. G. Garner, R. Allen and C. Short, 'Foot-and-Mouth Disease Vaccination: A Discussion Paper on its use to Control Outbreaks in Australia.' http://www.affa.gov.au/docs/animalplanthealth/chief_vet/fmdvac.htm

[39] Comments by Belgian and French farmers, reported in the broadsheets, Feb–March 2001

[40] 'Strategy for Emergency Vaccination against FMD, report of the scientific committee on animal health and welfare, 12/3/99' http://europa.eu.int/comm/dg24/health/sc/scah/index_en.html

To conclude:

It is clear that in MAFF's opinion, ongoing technological progress in vaccine development will never be sufficient to justify use in the field – this is obvious from the fact that its arguments against vaccination have changed little since 1950 despite tremendous scientific advance. In fact, MAFF has set completely unobtainable scientific criteria that supposedly justify its rejection of vaccination but actually just support its pre-existing decision not to vaccinate. The various logistical problems associated with vaccination could be overcome if MAFF had the will. Instead they are highlighted as reasons why vaccination could never work.

- The true reasons for not vaccinating are grounded in misplaced confidence that because slaughter has always worked in Britain, it will work again if applied with sufficient vigour. This ignores the huge national and international changes in the last 50 years which assist the spread of FMD, and the additional epidemiological knowledge which confirms FMD as the most contagious disease known to man.

- In addition there is the matter of national pride. Evidence from other nations shows far less ambivalence to vaccination; was MAFF to choose to vaccinate at this point this decision would be entirely justified in terms of EU policy. But MAFF feels that Britain is superior to vaccination, that only 'weak' or 'inferior' nations, unable to control disease properly, need resort to such technology. Ironically, scientific advance is presented as a backward step while application of nineteenth-century slaughter and burning is 'progress.' Britain spent the majority of the twentieth century boasting about its superior sanitary status and disease 'purity', achievable through stamping out. In the case of FMD, Britain encouraged the rest of the world to follow its example.[41] There are still the shreds of

[41] see various PRO MAFF files discussing the formation and actions of the European Commission on FMD

this national reputation at stake here, despite BSE and swine fever. MAFF probably feels that vaccinating would seal international opinion that Britain is 'the leper of Europe'.

- Since opposition to slaughter has historically always gathered pace over time as the policy has failed, MAFF probably feels that an intensive strike would wipe out the disease quickly and with it the public objections and ultimately public memories of the carnage. Turning to vaccination at this point when the decision could so easily have been made earlier without such extensive slaughter would seriously undermine MAFF's reputation and legitimacy. Also, in a sense, this would betray all those past CVOs who put their careers on the line to withstand farmers' complaints and assert that slaughter was the best and the only way to control FMD. The fact that slaughter of up to a million animals is supposedly justified in order to save a single government department's credibility can surely not be tolerated.

SUMMARY OF OVERALL FINDINGS

- Slaughter as a first line of defence against FMD invasion was introduced in an entirely different context to the present, on purely economic grounds. Those grounds are more justified today than in the past due to present agricultural practices and the globalisation of trade. However, the very fact that these conditions are open to change over time means one must guard against granting the slaughter policy a permanent status. Whilst the economic situation may justify slaughter, if that situation changes, the veracity of the policy is thrown into question. There is therefore a strong case for examining whether costs involved in the proposed mass cull (in addition to the consequential losses to farming and the tourist industry) may outweigh the costs to the export industry imposed by alternative methods of disease control.

- Slaughter has always eliminated FMD but on certain occasions, as at present, confidence in the policy has been severely shaken. History reveals that conditions associated with the present outbreak made the current state of affairs virtually inevitable. Criticisms of the slaughter policy made during extensive past outbreaks are still relevant today. Leaving aside the question of whether or not slaughter is at this point economically or morally justified, the feasibility of its practical implementation must throw a huge question mark over whether such a course should be attempted. It is important to realise that those opposing slaughter are not self-interested cranks any more than those supporting the policy, despite the fact that historically they have been portrayed as such. Additional motives and interests shape everyone's opinion on slaughter and should be taken into consideration when deciding upon its continuation.

- While vaccination does present technical and administrative difficulties, these could be effectively tackled were the Ministry to desire it. Instead, technical and practical problems are presented as almost insurmountable. It is important to realise that MAFF has never wanted to vaccinate and that the problems it cites merely justify an existing stance rather than providing its basic rationale. No vaccine will ever achieve the standards MAFF desires, and the reasons for this lie in the arena of national pride, historic tradition and government credibility to the public. MAFF hides deeper anti-vaccination sentiments behind scientific reasoning, and this deserves to be recognised. If the economic reasons for slaughter or its practical feasibility are thrown into question then vaccination is the only real alternative. The grounds cited by MAFF are insufficient for the rejection of vaccination and exposing the real reasoning behind this decision is necessary in order for any substantial challenge to be mounted against this decision.

- MAFF has grown powerful through the past elimination of FMD and through repeated victories against the critics of slaughter. Tradition plays a huge role in its approach to this disease problem and in the current critical situation, historical success is possibly the only certainty MAFF has left to cling on to. Here I have undermined that certainty and with it, many of the reasons for continuation of the slaughter policy.

TOWARDS A NEW
UNDERSTANDING

THE REALITY OF RURAL POVERTY

Caroline Hitchman

REAL POVERTY IN A MYTHICAL SETTING

POVERTY IN THE countryside has long been considered secondary to poverty in the town. Although the ongoing crisis in farming has probably helped to raise awareness of rural poverty, the countryside is all too often viewed in idyllic terms for its picturesque beauty, its closeness to nature and its open fields. Urban dwellers see it as a retreat for weekends or holidays; or dream of moving there when they have the money, when they get married, when they have children, when they retire, etc. They gauge the countryside in dreamlike terms.

Those who have been trying to prove the existence of rural poverty in the UK and get it on the government agenda have had a long struggle. The indicators for poverty used by the government have been criticised for having an urban bias. Rural poverty is dispersed over the countryside instead of being clustered in one locality. Visitors touring the country-side see the pretty houses along the road but not the isolated cottages, the gentrified ex-council houses but not the cramped row round the back. Urban dwellers visiting the countryside see what they want to see: nature, open spaces, a slower pace of life. The countryside is rarely viewed as it actually is. The more affluent rural dwellers themselves may not see the poverty in their own neighbourhood. This essay aims to guide the reader into thinking more about the shadowy nature of rural poverty, and about some of the different factors that contribute to its existence.

A research project carried out by Demos, the Henley Centre and Thames Valley University[1] examined access to food and reasons for food choice among low-income consumers in urban and rural areas. As its fieldworker I asked a small number of low-income families to keep two-week diaries of diet, time and money. I also conducted more than fifty in-depth interviews over a period of three months, collecting material from the Forest of Dean to set against nationwide research, mainly from the Countryside Agency's recent report, *The State of the Countryside*.[2] Points from this are quoted in the chapter, each marked with a bullet.

DEFINING POVERTY

'In nine out of the twelve areas, at least 20% of households were classified as being in or on the margins of poverty.'[3] So said a report in 1994. But how is the word 'poverty' actually defined and used?

There are two broad definitions: absolute poverty and relative poverty. Absolute poverty means not having enough resources to obtain the minimal means of survival (food, water, clothing, shelter, [perhaps] health care). Relative poverty was defined by the European Council in 1984 as meaning that people's 'resources (material, cultural, social) are so limited as to exclude them from the minimum acceptable way of life in the member state in which they live'.

This definition introduces the idea of social exclusion which the UK government has recently been concentrating on. Relative poverty is not just about income (by rule of thumb,

[1] Hitchman, C., Harrison, M., Christie, I., Lang, T., *Running on Empty: access to food on a low income*. Demos 2000 (publication forthcoming)

[2] *The State of the Countryside*. Countryside Agency, 1999

[3] Cloke, P., Milbourne, P. and Thomas, C., *Lifestyles in Rural England*. Rural Development Commission [now the Countryside Agency], 1994

50% of the average) but involves a complex series of factors. These factors include: access to opportunities, training, housing, education, social networks; experience of discrimination; sense of citizenship; health; and cultural/spiritual activities. Relative poverty leads to long-term failure to thrive; it may involve family breakdown and crime.

If we take income as the crucial factor, how are we to measure it and take into account all the variations? If we use the 1984 definition, what is 'the minimum acceptable way of life'? States may use their levels of national social assistance as the minimum. Who decides on these levels, on what basis, how are they uprated? If the benefit levels are raised, does that mean the number of poor people will rise?[4] What do people in a given society think constitutes a minimum standard of living?[5] Interestingly, those who fall into a survey's category of 'poor' or 'socially excluded' often do not consider themselves to be so.

THE FACTORS CONTRIBUTING TO RURAL POVERTY

The central point in rural poverty is *isolation*. Vulnerable groups such as the elderly (a larger percentage in rural areas), the handicapped, single parents with young children, and young people can easily fall into the category of the socially excluded if they do not have a car. An increasing lack of services at a local level does not just lead to social and cultural isolation but decreases the chances of finding employment as well as causing difficulties in terms of access to schools, health services, shopping, etc.

[4] Dowlett, E.A. and Dobson, B.M., Symposium on 'Nutrition and Poverty in Industrialized Countries'. See *Nutrition and Poverty in Europe: an overview*. Proceedings of the Nutrition Society 56 (1997): 51–62

[5] *Poverty: The Facts; Breadline Britain 1990s*. (Child Poverty Action Group)

Transport

Access to a car is now an essential component of rural life:

- 84% of rural households had a car (and 38% had more than one) compared with 69% nationally (and 25% with two or more)
- taking only low-income households (the bottom 10%), those living in rural areas were twice as likely to have a car as similar households in larger towns and cities.

These figures indicate the importance of having a car but also point to the problem for those who haven't. Increasing taxes on fuel hit the rural poor harder than anyone as there isn't usually a choice on cutting down journeys. Research in rural Scotland by Oxford University[6] (using a sample of 1,000 households in five rural areas) showed that in the lowest income group (less than £10,000 per annum), 37% of all households spent between £10 and £20 a week on motor fuel and 17% spent more than £20. In the second lowest group (£10–15,000) 38% spent between £10 and £20 a week and 36% spent more than £20. These are significant prices for low-income households. Cars tended to be smaller and older, therefore less fuel-efficient.

Those without a car are in the minority and are hit the hardest. A health visitor in the Forest of Dean summed it up when she said: *'If you haven't got a car you've had it.'*

One of the diary keepers was a pregnant, single mother with three children. She had not gone shopping for a fortnight: she was short of money, and the idea of going to the supermarket and carrying the bags home was too much. At least in these villages there were local shops, but the quality of the food may be poorer and the prices higher. Thus the poor pay more.

[6] Farrington, J., Gray, D., Martin, S., 'Rural Car Dependence and the Rising Cost of Car Use'. *Town & Country Planning* 66 (1997): 214–16

Public transport was poor:

- 75% of rural parishes had no daily bus service and 65% had no six days a week bus service
- where services existed, they were often limited: 44% of parishes had no service before 9 a.m. and 77% no service after 7 p.m.
- 93% of rural parishes had no rail service.

Buses were infrequent – once or twice a day – and activities had to be planned around the bus timetable. Evening activities without a car were impossible. '*Getting out of Cinderford is very difficult,*' said a boy of eighteen. '*Because of the cost, £1.70 and the last bus from Gloucester is 7.15. To get to Coleford, it's £2.25 and the last bus is at 8.45 p.m. The pictures start at 8.30 and I had some free tickets.*'

Shopping for many elderly people is an important, enjoyable activity of the week where they can go out, talk to people, get some exercise and have a chance to look around. When the bus back from town leaves at 11.25 a.m. instead of its previous time, 1 p.m., then as a seventy-five-year-old woman said, '*It's terrible.*' Why no consultation before such changes are made?

Even if the main route service was adequate, cross-country routes were much more difficult. Some key services were inaccessible by public transport.

'*There's no bus to the hospital,*' said a man of thirty-nine. '*I had to get a bus to Cinderford and then walk and then take a bus to Lydney and walk nearly a mile uphill to the hospital. We don't qualify for Dial-a-ride as we're not on income support.*'

The buses were frequently old coaches and the high steps made it difficult for older people to get on and off. There was little space to put the shopping. '*With a pushchair it's very difficult,*' said a twenty-one-year-old mother of two. '*You've got to try and get a child on and your shopping. Everyone is watching you as you get all your shopping on. My husband wouldn't want to go shopping when he comes home from work.*'

What about Internet home shopping? Surprisingly the majority said no. They liked to do their own shopping. *'It's the only place I go really,'* said a mother of five.

Public transport, particularly buses in rural areas, is a very difficult and complex area for policymakers. All too often the buses are practically empty. If the bus service was in high demand there would not be a problem. A number of community transport schemes are emerging across the country. Community-led answers, helped and funded by local councils, are the only solution.

- Community transport, though not widespread, has been expanding, and by 1997, 21% of rural parishes had some form of community minibus or social car scheme. Similarly, 15% of rural parishes had a Dial-a-ride scheme for people with limited mobility.

Services

A village shop can be one of the hubs of community life, a lifeline for those without cars, particularly the elderly. It provides not just food, drink and household items, but often a reason to go out and a vital source of human contact. One shopkeeper remarked that she felt more like a social worker at times.

- 42% of rural parishes had no shop, the actual number of food shops decreased by 4,000 in rural England from 1991 to 1997
- 70% had no general store
- 43% had no post office.

But the prices are higher. *'If I'm desperate I'll go to the local shop,'* said a single father, aged forty-five, *'but you can spend a tenner there without blinking an eyelid.'*

Other services, too, are in decline:

- 49% had no school (for any age)
- 29% had no pub

- 91% had no bank or building society
- 83% had no GP based in the parish
- 28% had no community centre

Financially it is more viable for services to be in main centres where they can serve a larger number of people; the smaller the village, the fewer the users. Some villages have clubbed together to buy their local shop, but in most the services simply disappear leaving the vulnerable at further risk.

- *Older people*: 91% of rural parishes had no day care; 80% no residential care; 61% no recreational clubs
- *People with disabilities*: 96% of rural parishes had no day care; 91% had no residential care for people with learning difficulties or physical disabilities
- *Younger people*: 50% of rural parishes had no school for six-year-olds; 90%, no school for twelve-year-olds; 96%, no school for eighteen-year-olds; 68%, no clubs for young people
- *Young children*: 89% of rural parishes had no post-natal clinic; 93%, no public nursery, and 86% no private nursery; 61%, no parent and toddler group; 59% no pre-school playgroup; 92%, no provision for out-of-school care
- Rural areas get less funding per resident for local authority services: schools, social services, libraries, concessionary travel and sports/leisure facilities.

The lack of amenities for young children, teenagers and young people was a particular problem mentioned in the Forest of Dean. This spiralled into other problems such as crime. *'There's nothing here, that's why the kids are such buggers . . . it does my head in, there's nothing round here'* (thirty-two-year-old mother of three).

Employment
The State of the Countryside report described how the rural economy was as diverse as the national economy with a similar

mix of industries and services. Rural districts have higher rates of part-time employment, self-employment and people working from home than nationwide figures. The rural workforce faces limited employment opportunities, low pay, job insecurity, little scope for career progression, a paucity of training and careers advice, a high degree of non-unionisation and a need to travel some distance to the workplace.[7] Between 1987 and 1997 over 60,000 farmworkers lost their jobs.

Employment in the Forest of Dean is dominated by manufacturing. There are some large companies (SmithKline Beecham, Rank Xerox) but generally the economy is dominated by small firms. In 1999 the unemployment rate in the Forest was 4%, lower than the UK average of 4.8% (99).[8] Approximately half of the interviewees were claiming benefits and half were in low-wage employment.

The search for better employment and better training drives young people out of the countryside. Many of the more talented, educated young are being lost.

INCOME AND COPING STRATEGIES

The mean household income of the respondents questioned regardless of age or family size was £103 per week. Shoppers usually had a keen awareness of the prices of goods in different shops and they could often quote prices to the penny. They had to be excellent managers of money as they managed a family on so little:

'I get a pension of my own from work. I think I'd be better off on income support, I get £150/month and an old age pension of £81/wk. From my pension come the bills: water £32/month; council tax £42/month; electric £40/month; TV £8/month – that leaves me £30/week to live on. From the other pension I pay £58/fortnight for the house and £15/wk

[7] Arkleton Centre for Rural Development Research, *Disadvantage in Rural Areas* (RDR 29, 1997). Rural Development Commission [now the Countryside Agency]

[8] Forest of Dean District Council, *An Economic Development Profile of the Forest of Dean* (1999)

for food. I don't manage to save but I don't go short,' said a man of sixty-nine.

Coping strategies become ways of life on a low income. Food was usually a top priority for families, comprising 34% of their total budget. When funds were short, luxuries were cut out: named brands, chocolates, cakes, meat and fruit.

'Many a time, I go without,' said a single mother of four, *'the kids don't, I do. If I've got to pay a lot out one week then I'll go short, the kids will all have meat and I won't. They might go without their crisps for school, they still have their fruit and veg, I ain't a big fruit and veg eater anyway.'*

The strong family networks were a huge support net to young families who were often the most vulnerable financially.

Catalogues were often used to buy clothes and household goods so that payments could be divided. It was very common for families to belong to clubs where money was put away each week for Christmas or a special occasion, planning often began months in advance. Others got into debt by borrowing from a loan shark; they charge extortionate rates of interest, but are often the only available source of money. More than 70% of the interviewees had no form of savings.

HOUSING

- There were nearly four million dwellings in rural England (20% of England's total housing stock), 5% built since 1991, the number of rural households in England was projected to increase by a million, 25% from 1991 to 2011. This growth would stem almost equally from within the existing rural population and from inward migration
- Of England's second homes, 58% were located in rural districts
- There was more owner occupation in rural areas, 74% compared with 67% nationally, and less social housing, 15% compared with 23% nationally
- Significant numbers of rural households were unable to become owner-occupiers locally and there was a shortage of social and affordable housing

- Two-thirds of households could not afford to purchase an appropriate-sized home, given their current incomes, according to one study
- There was an estimated need of 80,000 additional affordable homes in rural areas between 1990 and 1995; however, since 1990, only 17,700 had been built.

The lack of affordable housing is another reason for the loss of young people in the countryside as they cannot afford to set up home in their own area. Overall, two-thirds of those contacted by the Centre for Housing Policy at the University of York, researching this question, expected to leave their rural area.[9] Five issues concerned them:

1. *Availability*: little housing was suitable in either the owner-occupied or the rented sectors, much of it being family-sized.
2. *Affordability*: the costs of owner occupation were typically prohibitive, rents were high, and help available through the benefit system restricted.
3. *Access*: there were financial barriers (e.g., the cost of upfront rent deposits), status barriers (e.g., landlords' reluctance to accept those on Housing Benefit) and qualification barriers (young people not being a priority for social housing).
4. *Information*: little advice or help with finding accommodation was available locally.
5. *Condition*: some housing was in poor condition, especially in the private rented sector.

Not surprisingly these problems result in increasing rates of homelessness in rural areas. The homelessness is often hidden as people stay in friends' or parents' houses for long periods of time. However, the reports of people sleeping rough in

[9] Centre for Housing Policy, University of York, *Young People and Housing* (RDR 31, Rural Development Commission [now the Countryside Agency], 1997)

rural areas are increasing.

In the Forest of Dean, 90% of the respondents were from social housing. Frequent complaints were made about difficulties with the council if a family wanted to move. Two organisations which provided emergency accommodation for young people and abused women, housing advice and a limited number of flats, were highly valued.

WHAT SENSE OF COMMUNITY?

Many believe that the countryside still has the close society of the past, with a much more stable population of families who have lived there for generations. In the Forest of Dean this proved to be true in the main. Many communities had indeed been there for a long time, and often members of a family lived in the same village. But if relationships turned sour, these close environments could also be a problem.

Many elderly people and adults who had been brought up on the estates didn't think the community life was as it used to be. In one place, new social housing stock had been built, causing a relatively large influx of new people. Tensions arose between people whose families had lived there for generations and the incomers, or 'outsiders', who came to the area to live. Frequently the incomers would try to change things, bringing new ideas and wanting to influence the area in which they lived. One elderly ex-coal miner explained: *'Outsiders come in and spoil things by being argumentative.'*

The definitions of belonging were more stringent and historically peculiar in the Forest of Dean, as there were a certain number of people who were properly called 'Foresters'

But in many communities, incomers and Foresters lived harmoniously side by side, so long as the former group respected the difference and didn't pretend to be Foresters themselves. Changes had to be brought in slowly and with the agreement of a mixture of people. The same ex-coal miner also explained, *'once you've found a friend in a Forester, you've got a friend for life'.*

There were real difficulties on the council estates I visited: a sense of stagnation, a lack of privacy, an influx of problem families. But scattered cottages had problems too. An elderly lady I visited one afternoon in a small semi-detached cottage was often alone all day as the others in the isolated row of houses all went to work.

There were some community groups in the villages I visited: mother and toddler groups, the Women's Institute, old people's luncheon clubs, gardeners. But one young single mother didn't go to the mother and toddler group (associated with the church) because she felt everyone there had a husband and was looking at her. For minority groups, whether social or ethnic, the chances of social exclusion are much higher in a rural environment due to a lack of diversity (only 1% of ethnic minorities), antipathy to change and often quite conservative value systems still remaining.

CONCLUSION

Local Agenda 21 meetings look at local solutions to improve the quality of life. Organised by local government, they are meant to be inclusive and representative. One in the Forest of Dean was advertised on local radio, in local newspapers, etc., but the turnout consisted of the same familiar faces of well-meaning, hard-working professionals (including myself). There was a very poor turnout of Foresters or low-income households. But country people with no job, training, transport or opportunities, and little income, tend to be disempowered and isolated, they lack self-esteem and motivation. It will require considerable time, effort and money to involve them, but unless they themselves help to bring about changes, poverty will never be alleviated.

Awareness of rural poverty is a start; the next step is action. A love of the countryside must include its people. Rural industries need to be promoted, supported and enlarged. If an urban household wants to move to the country, could it take its work along, instead of commuting? Local employment opportunities are vital. Let us start appreciating the countryside for more than its weekend or holiday value.

THE RIGHT WAY FOR ANIMAL WELFARE: JUST HOW SHOULD WE RELATE TO ANIMALS?

Graham Cox

THE NATURAL WORLD is extraordinary. And daily, it seems, we are made more keenly aware of just how extraordinary it is. If, as we are told, chimpanzees share 98.9% of our human DNA and management theorists feel they can gain valuable insights into the nature of organisations from observations of ant colonies, then thinking clearly about our own obligations towards the natural world becomes both urgent and more challenging. For although our sense, albeit thoroughly secularised, of being part of a 'great chain of being' has never been more developed, we have never been less at ease about the implications of the place we suppose we occupy within it.

The seductions of a rights-based discourse are many. Indeed, the road from claiming that chimpanzees have similar capacities for thought and arithmetic as four-year-old children, and suggesting, as the Great Ape Project has done, that chimpanzees, bonobos, gorillas and orang-utans should be recognised as having rights to life, liberty and freedom from torture is easily travelled. But it is a primrose path and the journey is without any obvious destination. Genetic and behavioural evidence may encourage us to believe that the

137

moral respect and consideration that characterises distinctively human interaction should also characterise interactions between humans and apes. But, once we embark on an extension of the boundaries of morality in this way, there is no obvious place to stop. Ants might surely be thought worthy of respect, and bananas, with which we share 50% of our DNA, will doubtless have their advocates.

The scope for radical confusion is considerable. It is, moreover, a confusion which is inimical to the interests of other species. We can only give real meaning to notions of rights by invoking a series of associated concepts, the most significant of which is responsibility. And if we try to apply that concept to animals we quickly find ourselves mired in incoherence. Animals cannot properly be thought of as moral beings and the discourse of rights generates countless absurdities and paradoxes. We may wonder at the seemingly incredible, yet separately identifiable, number of notes which make up each second of a skylark's song without ever wishing to describe skylarks, or other songbirds, as good musicians. To do so would involve an inappropriate application of a moral concept which can only be rightly applied within the human sphere.

Rights can hardly be applied according to some sliding scale of sentience and mental capacity without, for instance, compromising the status of impaired human adults and young children who might find themselves considered less valuable than some animals in the light of such a scale. Indeed, it is surely no accident that the animals vigorously defended by those who strongly espouse the animal rights case are those which appeal most readily to the aesthetic senses and sentiments of humans. Michael Jackson's chart-topping paean to 'Ben' notwithstanding, brown rats have few defenders. This is despite there being a hierarchy of regard which is consistently apparent and which generally privileges warm-blooded furry animals over feather and fin. And if the animal has a 'baby face' and is capable of making something akin to facial expressions its chances of finding special favour are much enhanced. Though couched in the language of general principle, rights-based arguments tend, in practice, to be quite restricted in their range of application. Insects, though a vital element of the natural world and its food chain, feature hardly at all.

Quite aside from the absurdities and paradoxes with which it is inevitably associated, the animal rights position represents a chronic failure to come to terms with animals as they really are. As such it does them a disservice because the actions needed to further the interests of species are compromised by the attention accorded to individuals and their rights. Indeed, it needs to be emphasised that if the objections to animal rights argument from moral philosophy are significant, those which are rooted in an understanding of animal biology are even more profound.

None of this means, of course, that we do not have obligations of the most pressing kind towards the natural world. Our increased awareness of environmental relationships has, whatever else, emphasised that biodiversity and the well-being of that natural world is overwhelmingly dependent on us. Making such an observation does not commit us to some naïve and unacceptably paternalistic stewardship: it is simply to state the obvious. In almost every significant respect it is we who call the shots that really matter. For even the disasters which we call 'natural' are crucially mediated both before, during and after their occurrence by human intervention.

It follows from recognition of this mutual dependence that the proper care of animals, and acceptable attitudes towards them, are rightly considered moral obligations. And we are right, moreover, to consider an awareness of such issues a proper part of everyone's education and culture. So, although notions of animal rights can only be considered a snare and a delusion, a concern for animal welfare has to be nothing less than prominent in any society which aspires to being considered civilised.

Animals are not moral beings and it is, moreover, easy to see how the serious application of rights-based arguments would be inimical to their interests. Is every fox to stand accused of murder, for instance? Animal welfare is, however, another matter entirely and we have carefully to consider how we are to give practical meaning to the concept. Thought experiments have no place. Sentiment, and the fictions that depict animals in anthropomorphic ways, have similarly to be sidelined. Our concern for animal welfare must be rooted in a realistic assessment of other species and their needs. And that concern must be informed by rigorous and responsible science and the best field biology allied to a respect for habitats and for the natural order.

Good animal welfare, of domestic animals in particular, can be promoted by closely observing the reality of the animal world and learning from husbandry skills as they are practised by those who work with animals. Indeed, the best animal husbandry practices embedded within rural life are a key learning resource which needs at least to be preserved and, if possible, enhanced at this time of structural dislocation and transformation in agriculture and the countryside which is almost certain, otherwise, to prove inimical to animal welfare.

A realistic assessment of other species involves recognising that animals have neither human needs nor human expectations. Evolution and, in the case of domesticated animals, selective breeding over many generations have generated in each species characteristic needs and capabilities which are allied to the ability to withstand certain pressures. So it is unlikely, for example, that a wild rabbit would be as disturbed by being pursued by a fox as would a domesticated chicken. Escape by running is central to the rabbit's very nature. Welfare considerations should ideally, therefore, be specific to species. They must take account of stress and the adaptive response that determines whether it can be readily coped with from an animal's inherent repertoire of defences.

Stress, it must be acknowledged, is a notoriously difficult concept: not least because of the prevalent tendency to equate it with suffering. But the committed athlete, just as much as any hunted animal, experiences stress and the relationship of that stress to performance is complex rather than simply damaging. In the case of animals, who are unable to offer an assessment of their own situation, the effort to determine what is to count as stress in the negative sense is especially taxing.

Nevertheless, neither these difficulties, nor our clear obligation to take careful account of difference, need be seen as cutting across another obligation, which is every bit as clear, to seek to establish general principles in terms of which animal welfare might be furthered. The Farm Animal Welfare Council appointed by the Government has sought to define good animal welfare in terms of Five Freedoms and, though they were of course initially articulated with farm livestock in mind, the Council has noted that they can be applied to species that are culled or taken in the course of shooting, fishing and hound sports. Indeed, there is no reason why they should not be applied to the generality of animals.

The first of them, freedom from hunger and thirst, emphasises the need for ready access to fresh water and a diet to maintain full health and vigour. Freedom from discomfort, meanwhile, points to the need for an appropriate environment including shelter and a comfortable resting area. Thirdly, freedom from pain, injury or disease entails prevention or rapid diagnosis and treatment. The fourth freedom is the freedom to express normal behaviour by the provision of sufficient space, proper facilities and company of the animal's own kind. The fifth freedom, finally, is freedom from fear and distress by ensuring conditions and treatment which avoid mental suffering.

The Five Freedoms, though in no sense the last word on this most contentious of subjects, represent an important codification of priorities. Similarly the 1997 Treaty of Rome protocol on livestock transportation was significant for recognising farm animals as sentient beings capable of feeling pain or distress without in any way precluding the use of animals for human benefit. The 1999 Treaty of Amsterdam, meanwhile, acknowledged 'sentiency' and the welfare of animals must now formally be recognised in the implementation of EU legislation. This clear appreciation of the significance of implementation is very important. For whether the specification of general criteria has a positive impact depends on a whole host of factors: not least of which are high standards of husbandry and regulatory strategies which prove to be robust at the international as well as at the national level. Considerations of practicality will always have a bearing, but that is precisely why codified priorities are so important.

To make serious headway in furthering the health and well-being of animals we certainly have to think in an integrated way. We have, in short, to be guided by general principles. But we have, also, to be aware of the needs of distinct species. The dangers of oscillating in our thinking between the very particular and the very general are, therefore, only too real. If we are to think and act constructively about animal welfare issues it is as well to recognise that we relate to animals in quite distinct ways. So, while acknowledging that they are socially constructed terms which carry a heavy burden of cultural baggage, we might, nevertheless, wish to distinguish the cases of pets, domestic animals and wild animals. We can expect the implications of the key considerations embodied, for instance in the Five Freedoms, to be somewhat different in the three cases.

In thinking about pets we enter a domain in which anthropomorphism is rampant: and is routinely invoked even by those who, in their more detached analytic moments, would be the first to acknowledge its inadequacy as a basis for real understanding. Though the abuse of animals is clearly as prevalent as that between humans within the domestic sphere, notions of closeness and concern are inseparable from the concept of the pet. We apply to such animals the idea that their lives should, so far as is possible, be fulfilled. We do not think it absurd to speak of them realising their potential. Moreover, the lives of pets are typically so entwined with human activities that, whether by design or not, they acquire social competences. Although they may not be considered to be 'fully paid up', as it were, pets are effectively members of our own moral community and, as such, we should recognise that the obligations on both sides are special.

Domestic animals are used for specific purposes and here too we have thereby acquired special responsibilities. In fact the law distinguishes in various ways between domestic and wild animals so that it would not, for instance, be acceptable to destroy a seriously ill pet rat with poison, as is considered acceptable for wild rats. Neither is it acceptable to confine a wild animal in the same way as we often confine pets and livestock. The use of animals, for whatever reasons, may involve direction in the form of training: but no one should suppose that this, though it may on occasion take unacceptable forms, in and of itself entails suffering. On the contrary, animals that are the beneficiaries of generations of breeding with particular purposes in mind only become truly themselves when the framework which training provides gives direction to their lives.

Of course, neither the animals we use for sporting and other working activities, nor the animals we rear for food can be said to have chosen either their genetic profile or their vocation. But they are what they are and our obligations to them are in no way lessened because what they are is substantially the result of decisions made by long-dead generations. On balance, our obligation to enable them to fulfil their potential should far outweigh any counter-impulse to confer on them a token and necessarily unreal autonomy.

Cruelty is another matter entirely and our thinking about it is at the heart of a whole series of fiercely contested issues in animal welfare. The seminal Cruelty to Animals Act of 1911 defined cruelty as the infliction of unnecessary suffering but left open the question of what might or might not be deemed necessary. Clearly the confinement of pet animals, veterinary procedures, the rearing and transportation of livestock for food, shooting, fishing, hound sports, culling for conservation and management purposes and vermin control can each involve impositions on animals that might be thought to constitute suffering. Certainly the 1911 Act was never intended to compromise pet ownership or meat eating and it has always been our responsibility to define the limits of the acceptable.

Suffering involves the feeling of pain, injury or acute discomfort – whether physical or mental – but it is well-nigh impossible to generalise in any useful way about how to detect it. In defining the limits of the acceptable we have to give very careful consideration to what is necessary and proportionate to achieve whatever benefits may accrue. That, in turn, entails having a keen and well-informed appreciation of the way in which animals live in the wild and the way they react to natural artificial sources of stress. Only then can we begin to address issues of cruelty with the seriousness they warrant.

An unashamedly utilitarian stance does not, on principle, rule certain activities out of court. If we consider the vexed question of animals in medical and scientific research, for instance, we can acknowledge – to cite just a few of the many examples – the medical advances made substantially due to animal experimentation in such areas as the development of vaccines, organ transplants and life-support systems for kidney, heart and lung machines, while also wholeheartedly endorsing the three Rs' principle for the replacement, refinement and reduction in the number of experiments. Mice, to cite only the most obvious example, have been used to study, *inter alia*, cancer, heart disease, diabetes, obesity, birth defects, cystic fibrosis, muscular dystrophy, vision and blindness, hearing, epilepsy, brain injury and stroke and Alzheimer's disease. With virtually all human genes having mouse equivalents here is a case where constant vigilance and adherence, as far as is possible, to the three Rs' principle is perhaps especially called for. But such considerations apply with special force to scientific research *tout court* and scientists must be prepared to acknowledge more readily that their activities cannot plausibly be characterised as value free. Such a stance is invariably simplistic and it legitimates, moreover, an unwarranted abdication of moral responsibility.

Responsible science which actively seeks to avoid any exploitation of animals sees itself as engaged in a moral discourse. It will recognise, moreover, that although scientific procedures may help to determine what level of welfare an animal is experiencing as a result of human intervention, only ethical arguments can seek to resolve the extent to which the situation is acceptable and proportionate to the benefits which might accrue.

Such assessments have also to be made in relation to the live export of farm animals over long distances which has become a matter of acute concern. The transport of animals does not necessarily, of course, result in poor welfare. Horses, for example, arrive at race meetings and events in peak condition: often after thousands of miles of transport. Appropriate arrangements for transport need to be specific to species. Indeed, much has been done to define in law the acceptable distances, vehicle facilities, rest times and supervision which are consistent with acceptable welfare outcomes, and every effort now needs to be made to enforce them. As always implementation is critical. And whether or not the journey involves the crossing of a national boundary makes no difference in itself to the welfare considerations.

Judged against the criteria embodied in the Five Freedoms the lives of quarry species often compare very favourably with those of farm animals. Much depends on habitat quality of course, but given an agreeable and supportive environment their day-to-day existence can be entirely consistent with high levels of welfare. Clearly issues of stress and suffering arise at or near the point of death and those who take part in field sports emphasise the importance of the expeditious recovery and efficient dispatch of wounded game. Stress is invariably a part of normal biological function, in that it helps to activate the survival strategies that the animal has evolved. Wild animals that normally escape predators by fleeing will normally experience stress when faced with a predator. We should not, however, conclude that this stress will necessarily have adverse consequences for their welfare. Obviously the dispatch of a fleeing animal almost definitionally, to state the obvious, 'compromises its welfare', at the point of capture. But such an observation is hardly the most important one to make. More significant, surely, is to note that its nadir is typically short-lived and that is not something that can always be said for a journey to the abattoir.

The welfare of quarry species is of such obvious concern to those who engage in the sporting activities associated with them that we should at least recognise that the welfare calculus is a complex one. For those whose objections are entirely ethical there can, of course, be no question of there being a calculus. But such a position is unlikely to enhance either the welfare of quarry species, or indeed the integrity of their habitats. The record of field sports interests in managing the environment and maintaining key components of biodiversity, on the other hand, is long-established and the repository of knowledge about species and their natural history within the community is considerable.

A feature of all the key examples we might draw on when considering animal welfare is that we have no grounds for supposing that health and well-being can be advanced by letting matters take care of themselves. Time and again we are obliged to recognise that what we suppose is 'natural' has or has had, in some way, the hand of human contrivance upon it. We must not sidestep our obligations by peddling fictions about the supposed self-regulatory qualities of the natural world. Advancing animal welfare involves many things, beginning with an informed understanding of the distinct needs of different species. In all areas there is a scope for individuals to make a difference.

Standards, codes of behaviour and effective means of giving them practical expression clearly have a key role to play and the regulatory strategies associated with them have to be effective as well. In particular there needs to be greater pressure for the international enforcement of standards. We must, moreover, be prepared to revise such frameworks as necessary when new knowledge about species becomes available. The Five Freedoms and the three Rs are important very general guides to action. They also provide a basis for monitoring developments and, in the case of animals used in scientific experimentation for instance, we can be clear that some progress is being made. That qualification is needed because the most recent Home Office figures indicate that, while overall the number of animal experiments fell slightly, scientific procedures involving genetically modified animals rose by 14% in 1998–9 and experiments with larger animals generally increased. Those involving dogs, for instance, went up by 20% to 8,185.

Much can be done to increase visibility, accountability and the sense of responsibility which people have for the ways in which they relate to animals. Livestock farms, sporting estates and rural businesses involving animals should be as open as possible to visitors who might thereby have the opportunity to develop an understanding of animal welfare based on the realities of work with animals. Educational programmes on animal welfare could take advantage of this resource because it is clear, for instance, that people whose only contact with animals has been with pets can benefit enormously from studying animal life in different contexts.

Everything must be done to enhance and generalise the best standards of animal husbandry. Continual training for those who work with animals is vital, but it must be underpinned by a pervasive and actively nurtured culture of good husbandry throughout the relevant domains where humans and animals interact. In agriculture, in particular, the live-stock sector can be encouraged to embrace higher standards by more informative meat product labelling. These and other initiatives can be expected to have a positive impact in fast-changing contexts where the predominant forces would otherwise be likely to be prejudicial.

But, however we seek to effect change, our efforts need to be driven by a clear philosophy: a core ethic which encap-sulates the integrated approach which the serious engagement with animal welfare issues presupposes. Active management is central to it. And that has to be informed by a thorough appreciation of the natural history and biology of species. And if we are to discharge our obligation to secure, as best we are able, the health and well-being of species we will have to appreciate, in an ongoing and active manner, that one concept in particular must be embedded in our strategies: balance. Like the vast complex of relationships we try to capture in the single term biodiversity, animal welfare, properly conceived, is a question of balance. Animals cannot, with any coherence, be accorded responsibilities: but if animal welfare is to be furthered we will have to embrace ours.

References

Stephen Budiansky, *If A Lion Could Talk: How Animals Think,* London: Weidenfeld & Nicolson (1998)

Graham Cox and Tony Ashford, 'Riddle Me This: The Craft and Concept of Animal Mind', *Science Technology and Human Values,* Volume 23, Number 4, 423–438 (1998)

Mary Midgley, *Beast and Man: the roots of human nature,* Brighton: Harvester (1978)

Roger Scruton, *Animal Rights and Wrongs,* London: Demos (1996)

Stephen Tapper, Ed., *A Question of Balance: Game Animals and their Role in the British Countryside,* Fordingbridge: The Game Conservancy Trust (1999)

John Webster, *Animal Welfare: A Cool Eye Towards Eden,* Oxford: Blackwell Science (1994)

ACCESS: A RESPONSIBLE VIEW

Nick Way

THE OUTRAGED RESPONSE in the countryside to the announcement, in 1999, of the government's proposal to legislate for a right of access, on foot, to open countryside (mountain, moor, heath, down and registered common land), now enshrined in the Countryside and Rights of Way Act, obviously came as a surprise to some ministers, even though the government had been left in no doubt as to this likely reaction.

Why should that be so? Why does this controversy matter to the future of the countryside? And why shouldn't the countryside at last be opened up to walkers when – in the eyes of some – it has been unreasonably 'forbidden' to them for so long?

OPPOSITION TO A NEW 'RIGHT OF ACCESS'
Why Make the Countryside's Problems Worse?

The decision to impose access by compulsion gets under the countryside's skin because the government appears to place a predominantly urban preoccupation above the concerns of those who live and work in the countryside itself. While post offices close, diesel prices soar and local hospitals are threatened with closure, country people see the government allocating precious parliamentary time to a measure that promises no obvious benefit, economically or otherwise, to their communities, particularly to very hard-pressed upland farmers. To be fair, the government has also announced a number of measures to assist agriculture and rural development and has promised help for rural post offices and greater acknowledgement of the role played by local public services. Nevertheless, country people find it hard to see why, given the government's recognition of the acute difficulties facing many rural communities, it pursues a measure that exacerbates, not ameliorates, these difficulties.

The Interdependence of Country Activities and Interests

The use of the word 'right' is itself provocative, because it gives the impression, not least to walkers, that one interest – theirs – is supreme over all others. In singling out this right, the government denies the complexity and interdependence of the many elements that enable the countryside to work. Economic pursuits, such as farming, forestry and other rural businesses, are inextricably linked with the environment and with the rural communities they serve, even at local level. There may be a number of activities and interests on a single piece of land. For example, the successful economic management of a heather moor in the north of England – open countryside to which the right of access will apply under the government's Countryside and Rights of Way Act – may depend not only on livestock farming but as much, if not more, on shooting. It is these activities that provide the habitat not only for grouse or other game birds, but also for plovers, merlins and hen harriers. It is these economic activities that keep the hotels, pubs and garages going during the quiet winter months. And there are other interests too, such as quarrying or forestry, which must all be accommodated and reconciled.

The countryside is a mosaic of thousands of such interdependent activities, cemented together in an economic, environmental and social relationship. Transferring *rights* from land managers to walkers disrupts these activities, even to the extent of endangering their viability and the environmental benefits that flow from those activities.

No New Right Should Override Existing Rights

The government appears not to recognise the importance of these relationships, and to treat sensitive parts of the country-side as free open-air leisure centres, not as living ecological and economic systems. The suggestion that the countryside is there for the use of all, free of cost, has implications every-where, not only on open countryside. It gives the impression that there is no reason why people should not walk anywhere, even if the rights-of-way network is the more appropriate means to accommodate access within the many, varied and legitimate other uses of rural land. In short, 'right to roam' suggests that new rights can be awarded without attaching necessary constraints or without affecting existing legitimate rights. This cannot be so.

Practical Concerns

Irrespective of these problems of principle, the legitimate practical concerns of those who live and work on the land have yet to be met. Practical difficulties may be inconvenient, but they cannot be ignored.

Unrestrained dogs worry livestock and disturb nesting birds. The Game Conservancy's evidence indicates that lower populations of merlins and hen harriers survive on land where there is open access than where their habitat has been left tranquil. The government has yet to accept that the period for controlling dogs needs to be extended until the end of July.

There is *no restriction on night-time access*, with the result that farmers and owners will be up at night to see why their dogs are barking or what a strange light on the horizon may mean. The hazards of night-time access – the extra costs to the emergency services from responding to calls from injured walkers and the security risks – are out of proportion to the tiny demand from those wanting to walk in countryside in the dark. In any case that demand can be met through prior agreements. The Chief Police Officers support restrictions on night-time access, but the government appears adamant that the clamour of a few should be heard above the reasonable concerns of a great many.

The exclusion provisions prevent occupiers from closing access at weekends and bank holidays for legitimate land management reasons, such as lambing and important shoots, except by request and permission from others whose livelihoods are not directly affected – the non-statutory local access forum and the Countryside Agency.

There is as yet no commitment to providing *wardening services, access points or signing*, even though open countryside may extend to four million acres, and management will be critical to the practicality of open access.

THE FAILINGS OF THE GOVERNMENT PROPOSALS
Public Demand Unsatisfied

Nor did the government explore the level or nature of demand for access, before embarking on legislation. Independent polling (commissioned by the CLA for its submission to the government's consultation on access to the countryside [www.cla.org.uk/access]) reveals that the public does *not* hanker for blanket access to open countryside, but would prefer efforts to be directed to providing clearly way-marked routes, and especially nearer to where most people live. Nor does the wider public put access ahead of the needs of livestock farming or the environment.

This gulf between the government's proposals and public demand is vividly exemplified by the experience of Northumberland Estates. In 1998 the estate offered extensive open-access agreements on moorland, but the Northumberland and Tyneside local authorities responded that demand for such access had already been met in full, and that what the people of Newcastle wanted was circular paths near to the city and in the wooded valleys of the Tyne. New paths were offered in these areas, but the negotiations were halted while the authorities waited for the government's announcement. The result of the government's decision is that the efforts of both sides will now be diverted away from this positive initiative to preparing for open access on the moors, for which there is little or no unsatisfied demand.

The Need for Management Unfulfilled

When meeting the representatives of other groups interested in access – the horse-riders, cyclists, orienteers, mountaineers and even the four-wheel drivers – the CLA has found that these groups did not ask to be given supremacy over others. The growth of all these pursuits, sometimes in conflict with each other, further demonstrates the need for management of access activities. The impression given to the rural constituency, however, is that the government is not aware of the diversity of these interests, or of the need for access management and for practical safeguards to protect existing livelihoods.

The Removal of Owners' and Occupiers' Rights

The legislation also raises legal questions about the occupier's liability and about the Human Rights Act. As the Act stands, a walker who falls and injures himself on a man-made feature of the landscape, such as a drystone wall (damaging the wall in the process), may claim compensation for his injury from the owner! Furthermore, the bill transfers rights, without consent or compensation, from property owners and occupiers, to walkers. Owners and occupiers will bear increased management costs on land of reduced value, with the overall costs amounting to up to £50 million per year. So far the government has declined to publish the advice it has received on the compatibility of this part of the bill with the Human Rights Act, and seems intent on fighting the battle in the courts. This atmosphere of fait accompli is compounded by the government's decision not to publish advice given to it on the environmental implications of the Act, by its own environmental advisers, English Nature. Such an approach defies the reality that successful implementation of the Act will depend on mutual cooperation and trust between owners, walkers, local authorities and English Nature itself.

POLICYMAKERS' MYTHS

But does this issue really matter to the future of the country-side? Yes, because apart from these important practical considerations, it symbolises the extent to which policy-makers do not see the real countryside at all, but base their decisions on perceptions that are more myths than realities: the myth that farming is in terminal decline, although farming will remain central to the future of the countryside, as provider of food, jobs and incomes, as the mechanism for stewardship and as the backdrop for tourism and inward investment; the myth that the countryside is well-off and the only support it needs can be provided through public sector and central government action, although in reality the lowest county GDPs per head are in Cornwall and the Isle of Wight; the myth that National Parks do not belong to anyone in particular, although in reality they comprise thousands of individual properties and livelihoods; the myth that the environment is a gift, for enjoyment by the public free of charge, but to be protected and paid for by someone else, although in reality conservation depends on an economic use for land and buildings.

How can we move away from the mythology to an approach on access that reconciles different interests, does not set town against country and meets public demand without compromising the needs of rural business or the environment?

HOW TO MAKE A 'RIGHT OF ACCESS' WORK

The Countryside and Rights of Way Act has now become law. Although the case for access by voluntary agreement remains strong it will be the new law that defines the terms on which access to open countryside is provided.

For access to work, the Countryside Agency and the Countryside Council for Wales, access groups, rural land managers and local authorities must have a practical and flexible framework in which local land management needs are fully respected. The 'right' to access must not be implemented anywhere before the needs of other existing interests in the countryside have been properly accommodated, or before adequate resources for access management have been provided.

The government and its agencies will need to accept the complexities of land management. Some general principles should be observed:

- Access policy should be founded on the realities of the countryside not the myths. That means listening to those who live and work there, putting practicality before wish lists; and means the government committing itself to fund access management adequately.
- Priority for opening access should take into account assessments of public demand and the relative costs of providing access in different areas – a cost-benefit approach.
- Access should not be introduced until all possible steps have been taken to remove practical difficulties. Where these are insuperable, access should not be a priority.
- Arrangements for access should remain flexible to take account of changing public demand or land management needs.
- Opportunities for local communities and affected land managers to benefit economically from the provision of access should be considered positively; for example, through the siting of car parking and advisory access points.

This approach does not, of course, remove the need to make major changes to the Act to tackle the practical difficulties already described.

Curiously, the provisions in Part II of the Act, for modernising the rights-of-way network, already embrace much of this more constructive approach. These have their origins in the pragmatic thinking of broadly based alliances of non-political organisations rather than in a campaign to achieve a symbolic objective.

In time, the positive approach embraced in the provisions to modernise the rights-of-way network could be extended to the management of access over open countryside, by transforming the 'right to roam' into a series of agreed practical arrangements for managed access. That, unfortunately, is only a hope, not a prediction.

DWINDLING HOPES OF RECONCILIATION

The atmosphere could be further improved if the government's Rural White Paper were a charter for its rural constituency, just as the Urban White Paper will champion the cause of its urban counterpart. Sadly, it is not.

However, if the government now proceeds to implementation without adequate resourcing and without heeding the warnings from those who are intimately involved in the practical management of our open countryside, then the prospects for a reconciliation on access are grim, and the consequences will be felt not only in the uplands but throughout the country, while the opportunity for a breakthrough in providing new access in the lowlands – where most people live – will be lost.

The outcome on access to the countryside is also linked with the government's wider rural policy. The rural constituency is unlikely to put the right to roam to one side in its general assessment of the government's performance, unless a much more reconciliatory and flexible approach is adopted, and unless the government's other rural policies tackle their particular and pressing needs.

Access to the countryside is, of course, not the only issue that matters to its future. Policies on agriculture, enterprise, the environment and the availability of services to rural communities are equally important. But any government that overrides the concerns of those who live and work in the countryside when implementing access policies will have considerable difficulty in persuading those rural communities that it has their interests at heart.

BRINGING THE COUNTRYSIDE
TO THE TOWN

Dawn Goodfellow

PROTECTING THE COUNTRYSIDE THROUGH EDUCATION

LIFESTYLES TODAY HAVE divorced the majority of the populace from any connection with the land or farming. The change in the structure of rural communities, the demise of the agricultural industry and the hysterical reaction to issues such as BSE and Genetically Modified Organisms need no expansion here. But how have we reached the current state of affairs where we have a country in which approximately 10% of the people live on 90% of the land?

While there is more leisure time than ever before, an increasing number of young families spend it in giant, out-of-town shopping malls rather than on Sunday afternoon walks. Children are not allowed to walk to school or spend happy hours playing in parks and on river banks because parents are terrified, by high-profile media stories, that they will be abducted. Family holidays are more likely to be taken in Tenerife or Florida than Devon or Wales. We no longer shop in small butchers' shops with carcasses hanging in full view, but in large superstores where meat comes in cellophane-wrapped packages that bear no resemblance to anything that might ever have lived. For the majority of families, their only contact with live animals is with pets. All these factors have contributed to a lack of understanding not just of our countryside, but, more fundamentally, of our relationship with animals, domestic and wild.

HOW CAN UNDERSTANDING BE INCREASED?

The Countryside Foundation for Education was started in 1986 by a group of country people who felt that many of the controversies and myths about the way that our countryside is managed resulted from a widening gap between rural and urban populations. It took some time for an effective plan of action to be developed. Research undertaken in 1992 examined what was being taught about rural issues within the state-maintained education system. It also examined teachers' attitudes towards the countryside and their perception of its relevance in modern education. That research revealed a fundamental lack of knowledge and understanding about the countryside and a lack of resources that would help to provide either that knowledge or ways in which it could be used in the education of young people. It also highlighted the number of single-issue lobby groups with interests in both built and global environments providing materials and support for teachers.

In the intervening eight years, the Countryside Foundation for Education has pursued a policy of producing very high-quality teaching materials about a whole range of rural issues and providing the training to enable teachers to use those materials effectively in the context of the National Curriculum. A number of other related organisations, such as the National Farmers Union, have also begun to take up the task. However, it is an uphill struggle, made more difficult by the numbers of different interest groups, from particular sectors of industry to environmental lobby groups or health education.

THE CRUCIAL ROLE OF TEACHERS IN SCHOOLS

The majority of teachers (even those working in rural schools) now come from urban backgrounds and those that don't almost certainly will have been trained by someone who has.

Again, like the majority of the population they have certain preconceptions about agriculture as a low-tech, outdated industry and the countryside as a place of leisure. Many of them view the countryside as irrelevant to modern children. The lack of personal knowledge of the subject, coupled with no training in how to use it as a resource for learning, means they do not feel confident in dealing with the subject and therefore avoid it.

The Countryside Foundation's contacts with teachers, through general marketing and teacher-training, suggest that the picture may, surprisingly, be even worse in rural schools than it is in urban. Frequently teachers in rural schools assume that their children 'know all about the countryside' and therefore need not be taught about it in the classroom. But rural communities are now more likely to be populated by town commuters than by farm workers, so that even people living in them have little or no idea about managing the land around them and the consequences of that management. Those few children from homes with one or both parents working in land-based industries are thus deprived in school of the opportunity to value their background and heritage, or to see it given status by someone as important as their teacher. While many schools, particularly in inner-city and deprived urban areas, emphasise the use of their funding to engender in children a sense of responsibility and value for their school grounds and local environment, we are devaluing that same sense of place for children living in some of the most beautiful parts of our country.

No teacher-training institution in this country has offered training about teaching any rural subject since the 1970s. This is another powerful message that rural issues are no longer of any relevance in our education system or our society as a whole.

The countryside community has been quick to attribute left-wing leanings to teachers and to provide anecdotal evidence of anti-farming or anti-country sport views taught in schools. In reality the reasons for this, where it has occurred, have been more about ignorance or indifference on the part of the teacher and the lack of readily available material expressing the equal and opposite view.

In recent years, since funds were allocated to individual schools to be spent as they considered most appropriate for their individual needs, school governors have become much more powerful in dictating what the school shall provide as a balanced curriculum. Each governing body (in a school above a certain size) should have some representation from local business on it. Few have included representatives of the land-based sector. Therefore, there is rarely much knowledgeable support from this influential body for a balanced portrayal of countryside issues.

WORKING WITHIN THE NATIONAL CURRICULUM

Since the advent of the National Curriculum, many teachers have struggled to cope with additional demands and restrictions.

When the National Curriculum was first introduced, it was far more prescriptive about the content of what teachers were expected to teach than had been the case before. The subsequent recognition that it was perhaps too prescriptive and that there was indeed too much content led to the adoption of a more 'context-based' approach. While teachers have more opportunity to develop their own methods of delivering the subjects, many of them still feel 'besieged', with no time to cover anything not specifically mentioned within the National Curriculum. Their own lack of knowledge about the countryside means that they cannot see that an infinite number of examples could be drawn from farming and the countryside through which they could teach many subject areas.

WHERE DOES THE COUNTRYSIDE FIT IN THE CURRICULUM AND NATIONAL EXAMINATIONS?
School Farms

The number of schools with a 'school farm', an area where children could experience close contact with animals and growing plants, has declined dramatically in recent years. As school budgets were 'squeezed', what was seen as a relatively high-cost item was a very early casualty. In a limited number of cases senior management and colleagues from other subject areas such as mathematics and English have recognised the benefits to children, of all abilities, of using the farm as a context for learning. In some other secondary schools staff or senior management have seen the potential of using the facility to support work with feeder primary schools or the community. In such cases the farm has become very much the hub of the school and brought great kudos to the school in question. However, these instances have been very much the result of the vision and enthusiasm of individuals and not because of support from government, local or national, for such development. Their sustainability then depends on those individuals, rather than on their being an integral part of a policy or strategy.

Syllabus Restrictions

Another casualty, which has itself contributed to the demise of many school farms, has been the examination syllabuses for 16+ students relating to agriculture, horticulture and rural science. The advent of the National Curriculum and the enshrinement in law of the subjects that students must study for the entirety of their statutory schooling have dramatically reduced their choices. Unless a subject has an examination/qualification at the end of it, it is likely to have no status within the school system. In addition, the examinations relating to agriculture and horticulture are seen as expensive to run and taken by relatively few students. So large numbers of schools no longer offer the subjects.

In 1984, 18,000 students entered for examinations in rural subjects, in 2000 there were less than 1,800. There are now only two examination syllabuses on offer at GCSE level, those of Agriculture and Horticulture offered by AQA (Associated Qualifications Authority) and Rural Science offered by OCR (Oxford, Cambridge and RSA Examinations); and in a recent review of the GCSE syllabuses that schools are able to offer students, it was recommended that the former be abandoned on the grounds that there were similarities to the latter. However, the motives behind the abandonment are very questionable. The examination boards are themselves commercial entities, therefore to run an examination that is entered by relatively few is in itself not a good commercial proposition. While in itself it may affect small numbers of students, it merely contributes to the downward spiral of all things rural within the curriculum.

The Agricultural Colleges

The nature of agricultural colleges has changed substantially in recent years. Again they reflect the change in attitude towards our countryside and the farming industry. In the past, many of them had excellent relationships with the schools within their authority, providing trips to the college farm and an input at school events such as careers evenings. Following the 1992 change in the way they were funded, many could no longer afford to provide those services. Equally, they began to move away from courses about agriculture towards courses that had a broader appeal to young people, such as floristry, equestrianism and countryside management. Many of them have even changed their titles to exclude the word 'agriculture'. While one could argue that these changes reflect, to some degree, the changing nature of our countryside as a whole, equally it could be argued that they represent the view that our countryside is purely a place for leisure – some sort of theme park to be visited on a summer Sunday afternoon.

Can the Countryside Sector and Farmers Help Our Schools?

The countryside sector itself was slow to recognise the opportunities offered in working with education to equip teachers, students and parents with a far better understanding of the rural environment and the way our land is managed.

Many individual companies and sectors of industry long ago recognised the importance of the consumers, employees and decision-makers of tomorrow having an understanding of industry and the place of wealth creation within our society. Since the early 1980s they have been working with educationalists to develop sophisticated, effective programmes which promote economic and industrial understanding, in some cases environmental awareness, and of course a sympathetic profile for themselves with a particular age group. They recognised the human resource implication of a demographic downturn and saw that tomorrow's employees would need far higher levels of skill and the knowledge and attitudes that would allow them to change career perhaps a number of times throughout their working lives. Some large companies wished to be seen as 'good corporate citizens' in communities where they were the major employer.

Very few examples of companies or interest groups with a countryside focus engaged in such activity until relatively recently. These industrial parties were in a position to invest substantial resources in their efforts and are perceived in many cases to be high-tech, exciting enterprises. Land-based industries are a long way behind. They are made up of small enterprises that do not have the necessary financial or human resources. The number of people employed in land-based industries has declined dramatically and so there has been no concern over recruitment, although that is perhaps changing. Traditionally the sector has been made up of primary producers who, until relatively recently, did not perceive the need to market their products.

As I mentioned earlier, a number of single-issue lobby groups have been working with education. In the field of rural education these come particularly from the 'green' environmental and animal rights organisations. Many of them are extremely well-funded, powerful organisations that tend to hold very 'protectionist', and in some cases extreme, views that often take little account of the economic realities or the difference between preservation and conservation. Their materials have been well received by schools, generally not because of any particular political leanings on the part of teachers; they are high-quality educational materials produced by professionals, and the organisations have promoted and marketed them well to teachers who did not know that materials expressing equal and opposite views existed.

In recent years, as a result of pressure on farming incomes and, in a few cases, a genuine desire to share a passion for farming and the land, a proliferation of farmers have, through 'farm attractions', opened their doors, on a commercial basis, to the public. In many respects this is a positive move that gives many families their first experience of farming and the countryside, in an environment where they feel safe and comfortable. It can also provide schools with a local resource to replace a school or college farm that has been lost.

However, I have visited many of these farms and talked to the farmers who own and run them. The degree to which those farmers have had to 'sanitise' the experience to make it acceptable and attractive to the paying public is disturbing. The successful open farms that are visited by a large number of people every year are not representative of commercial farms, where livestock is openly reared, in even extensive conditions, for the purposes of meat production, but rather glorified petting zoos where animals have names and are fed titbits by the public. There is no sign of mud and muck and certainly no mention of death!

We cannot blame the farmers for this; they are merely catering to their paying customers in a commercial enterprise. And they are providing, for many families, a first experience of a safe, open green space or the opportunity of standing in close proximity to a large farm animal.

There is much to be learned from the experience of open farms, but it has little to do with the realities of farming our land to feed ourselves.

What Government Support Has There Been?

There have been some government-funded programmes and initiatives concerned to increase school visits to farms. The two most notable have been the Farmlink Scheme, organised by the Groundwork Trust, and the Educational Access element of the Countryside Stewardship scheme. Both schemes were initiated by government departments and agencies, with no consultation with, or input from, the Department for Education and Employment, or the Qualifications and Curriculum Authority (QCA), the statutory body with responsibility for the curriculum. Consequently they are seen to have limited relevance to schools and as a result have an equally limited take-up.

The Educational Access element of the Countryside Stewardship scheme offers farmers very small additional grants for providing public access for organised educational visits. In order to claim these grants they must produce an information leaflet about the farm, or particular aspects of it, and receive a certain number of organised visits per year. The grant is so small that it is uneconomic to even spend the time putting the information together. More importantly, training and support for the farmer is lacking. There is frequently a mismatch between what the farmer expects and what the educational groups (or the wider community) might need to find. Again, the lack of proper funding for the information leaflet and of any training on how best to put it together means that the presentation is frequently poor, reinforcing the perception of farming as a low-tech, old-fashioned industry. There are of course notable exceptions to this, such as farmers who have produced their own websites, but at the moment there does not seem to be any organised attempt to share such skill and practice.

Schools' Problems

There are a variety of reasons for the low take-up by schools. The main one cited by teachers and their colleagues is the cost. Yet some other children's attractions across the country charge very significant entrance fees but do not seem to suffer from the same problem. In many cases they are inundated by schools wishing to visit. More relevant are the logistics of taking children on visits to the countryside. The very cosy indoor life that many children lead now means that they do not possess such things as wellingtons or waterproof coats, and parents are not happy to see their offspring return with expensive trainers covered in mud!

Then, too there are health and safety implications. Sensational stories in the press about outbreaks of *E. coli* infection emanating from farm visits make both schools and the local education authorities very wary indeed about promoting such visits, in the same way that Outward Bound activity has suffered so much as the result of one or two isolated accidents. Contrast this opportunity, now, with the purpose-built, all-singing, all-dancing children's museum down the road whose beautifully produced brochure lands on the teacher's desk. The coach drops the teacher and thirty children at the door. Once inside there is little need for a 'risk assessment' – the pupils are going to be in a contained, safe environment all day with no opportunity to get wet or muddy or fall over in something unsavoury! Better still, the museum's education officer has prepared a series of activities, all connected to the National Curriculum subjects that the teacher has to teach.

Which would you choose?

WHERE DO WE GO FROM HERE?

There seems to be general agreement across both urban and rural communities that we have, on our small island, one of the most diverse and beautiful landscapes anywhere in the world. The enormous support that organisations such as the National Trust and the Royal Society for the Protection of Birds enjoy, with membership bases of millions, suggests that there is very substantial interest in both our rural culture and heritage and our wildlife. The will to save and nurture is there. But we must ensure that we are realistic about what we have and that decisions we make about our countryside are made by a population that understands the consequences of those decisions. We need to harness the interest and enthusiasm of our majority urban population into a genuine desire to learn about our living, working countryside and all its many different constituent parts.

The changing face of our agricultural industry, and the need to provide financial support for our countryside in a different way, offer us a great opportunity to do just that.

Some farmers are in a position to consider diversification and increasing public access; we should identify the training and skills they need just as we have supported other industries and workforces going through great periods of change. There should be extensive marketing, through farmers' own networks and organisations, of appropriate courses that carry some financial incentive to attend. This cannot be done in isolation, however, and requires, in current jargon, some 'joined-up thinking'.

The Countryside Agency currently has responsibility for promoting public access to our countryside and yet has no responsibility for educating the public. To believe that simply encouraging people to go out into the countryside will automatically increase their understanding of it is naïve. What it does is to increase their understanding of what they like about it rather than the reality of how country people have shaped it over the millennia. While the agency currently runs or promotes a number of courses for countryside professionals, these are, in the main, about development for the 'converted'. We need a variety of different ways of accessing a wide range of training and information for a number of different target groups.

The Department for Education and Employment, the QCA and the Office for Standards in Education (Ofsted) determine what will be taught in our schools, how it will be taught and how its effectiveness will be measured. Unless any one area of interest is seen as a priority by one or all of these bodies, schools will not perceive it as relevant. In recent times the government has given more support to, and placed more emphasis on, Education for Sustainable Development. The Council for Environmental Education, the umbrella body for organisations with an interest in this field, is gaining considerable influence in government circles. While in some respects this is to be welcomed, there is a danger that we will be faced with an old problem, i.e. that global and built environments are taking precedence over any reference to rural Britain. This body is in fact being driven, in the main, by the major 'green' environmental lobby groups and has very little representation within its membership from genuine farming or countryside interests. Thus, while Education for Sustainable Development offers huge opportunities to increase the profile of our countryside and its development, chances to promote a greater understanding of that countryside as a living, working environment are currently being missed.

QCA and Ofsted are in a position to influence what is taught in schools, both by insisting in their guidance for schools that within the curriculum there is specific reference to rural Britain and by producing case studies for teachers to illustrate how this can be achieved in a whole range of subjects. Within the framework for the inspection of schools, a number of quite specific issues are cited and commented upon; for example, the school's links with the wider community. Including a criterion, therefore, which questioned 'Where within the whole school curriculum are issues relating to rural Britain and its constituent industries considered?' would improve the countryside's status with senior management in schools.

Our countryside is in danger of being lost for ever through a fundamental lack of understanding on the part of the majority of our population of how it has been developed over time. Even more worrying than that same majority taking active decisions about the way we manage the countryside is the greater danger of apathy and indifference towards it. People simply want good-quality, cheap, readily accessible food at any time of year. They do not care where it comes from, or how it was produced. We must, therefore, educate people about the *whole* context of the countryside and its economic and environmental significance to our society. If we do not succeed in doing that, we will destroy rural communities and a landscape that has been loved and tended by generations who knew and understood it.

A COUNTRYSIDE FOR ALL

Michael Sissons

THE DYSFUNCTION BETWEEN town and country in Britain at the start of the twenty-first century is surely unique. Nowhere else in the developed world, not in France, Germany or Italy, not in Australia, New Zealand, or Canada above all not in the United States, are the tensions and misunderstandings between town and country which now characterise British domestic politics apparent.

In America the state of Wyoming, with a population of 480,000, sends two senators to Washington as does New York with a population of 18 million. In France a brand-new Countryside Party can win up to 12% of the vote in the centre and the south-west. In the region of Lazio in Italy the rural vote can and does overturn a decisive urban majority in Rome. Yet here a rumbling anger and bitterness echo from Caithness to Cornwall, a community of feeling that the rural vote and the rural voice have become marginalised and are no longer of any account. According to the NFU, 23,800 jobs in farming were lost in 2000. That is over one in twelve of the full-time non-family workforce. For many livestock farmers the outbreak of foot-and-mouth disease will prove the last straw. The anger and bitterness is exacerbated by a government which, while it uses the clichés of inclusiveness, has seemed for most of this Parliament obsessed with portraying the concerns of the countryside as strident and extremist. Matthew Parris wrote recently: 'The figure I seek is that part of our population which, were the impression to arise that the Government dislikes "these country people", might conclude that this means them. I should put the figure between four and eight per cent of the population.' In politics and the media, it seems to me, there is no longer any disagreement that this dysfunction exists. There is argument about why it has happened, who can be held responsible, and above all whether it matters.

There is equally little doubt that this is a recent phenomenon. The words of Blake's 'Jerusalem' carried a potent political message well into modern times, certainly up to and beyond 1945. The notion that the farmed countryside, the hills and moors, the seaside provided for the industrial masses both healthy recreation and spiritual balm was common political territory. Maybe the locals usually voted Tory and the visitors Labour, but there was shared satisfaction as to what the countryside provided for everyone.

In 1945 there were particular reasons for town and city dwellers to think well of the countryside. The recruitment posters had invoked a vision of rural Britain. This is what we were fighting to protect. Hundreds of thousands of city children had been evacuated to escape the Blitz. While many found this at first strange and even frightening, it seems that the overwhelming majority returned home at the end of the war with an affinity and affection for rural life which never left them. Moreover it could be seen beyond doubt that the countryside had responded magnificently to the challenge to feed Britain during the submarine blockade. 'Dig for Victory' was the most famous, perhaps the proudest, slogan of the war.

The Labour government of 1945 recognised this to the full, and as an economically crippled Britain pulled itself up by the bootstrings in a harsh and austere peacetime, the political messages to the rural population were embracing and reassuring. In Hugh Dalton's first Budget speech as Chancellor in 1946, there was a panegyric, moving then if somewhat ironic now, invoking the magic of the British landscape. 'We have a great wealth of natural scenery. There is a wonderful incomparable beauty in Britain – the hills, moors, downs, woodlands. There is beauty and history in all these places.' Tom Williams, a Yorkshire miner with a 33,000 majority in the Don Valley, was Attlee's Minister of Agriculture. His heart was in the job, and he proved a resounding success. He, with Attlee, Dalton, Bevin, Bevan, and virtually all the Labour Cabinet, marched into the lobbies in 1948 to defeat an anti-hunting bill. During this period came two pieces of legislation which were to define the shape of modern rural Britain: the Agriculture Act of 1947, which established the principle of support for farming; and the Town and Country Planning Act of the same year, designed to protect green-belt land from development.

In broad terms this consensus lasted through four post-war decades. I mean by this that if we consider any parliament before the 1990s, a nationwide movement of rural discontent as it exists now would have been inconceivable. I suggest that the first public manifestation of urban hostility towards the countryside arose in respect of the CAP, which proved far less popular than the traditional deficiency payments, which kept the price of food low, fanned anti-EEC sentiment, and, like the old Corn Laws, seemed to set interests of country and town on a collision course.

I became involved in rural campaigning at the beginning of the 1990s, virtually by accident and because I work in the media. The issue that ignited the rural fuse was of course hunting, on which I will not dwell. But the chemistry behind the decision to form a pan-countryside alliance, which led to the formation of the Countryside Movement under Sir David Steel's chairmanship in 1995, and then to the Countryside Alliance in 1997, is a more complex story. The second reading of the McNamara Private Members' Bill to abolish hunting in 1992 was a close-run thing. To the consternation of the Conservative Party the pro-hunting majority on a January Friday was just twelve. We had been running advertisements in the broadsheets publicising the names of a wide variety of people from all walks of life who were prepared to support hunting. In the ensuing conversations, we found to our surprise that invariably a much wider feeling of dismay and apprehension about the problems of the countryside in general was coming to the surface. We resolved to conduct detailed polling in rural areas, which was done in advance of the Countryside Movement launch in 1995. There was, it became apparent, a huge throbbing rural boil out there. Over 80% of those polled believed that rural people had lost control of their destinies, that there was a great and growing gulf between town and country, that townspeople simply didn't understand the countryside, in effect that the town had come to dislike and even despise the countryside. We also filmed interviews in London about attitudes to rural life. Graven in my memory is the Lambeth hairdresser who, when asked where milk came from, could only answer 'Tesco'.

Here, it seemed, was a truth that all three parties were missing. The Liberal Democrats, torn between their urban and rural identities, were reluctant to court controversy on rural issues, although most of their rural MPs were quick to nail their colours to the countryside mast behind David Steel's example. The Conservatives, quite simply and not surprisingly, took their rural constituency for granted. For the Labour Party rural issues in opposition had been just about as low on the political agenda as it was possible to be without dropping off the scale. This was the first Labour Shadow Cabinet in which there were no credible experienced figures whatsoever to hold the rural, agricultural and environmental portfolios. The last Minister of Agriculture in the Callaghan government, Cledwyn Hughes, a countryman to his boots, became a founding director of the Countryside Movement. Ironically, in view of the massive rural disaffection that has arisen in this parliament, Labour were warned loud and clear in opposition in 1995 by the rural lobby that the problems of the countryside went far beyond the hunting issue. Their reaction was dismissive. A number of vocal Labour MPs, Elliot Morley, Tony Banks, the late lamented Ron Davies among them, received financial support from animal rights groups and sought to identify rural protest with field sports. Morley, in a phrase that has returned to taunt him, branded hunting supporters 'a tiny and reviled minority'. When Labour won the 1997 election, there were no policies in readiness for the countryside, not for the future of agriculture, not for the preservation of the landscape, not for the rural economy.

But this is not to blame Labour alone for the dysfunction which had by now arisen. Far from it. For Labour had only to look at the Conservative agenda to see that the countryside didn't seem to matter politically. And here is the paradox at the heart of the matter. Tony Blair came to power preaching inclusiveness. Yet he inherited a country which was compartmentalised by the pollsters, the spinners and the focus groups in response to the dictates of modern politics. A simplistic evocation of a united Britain as Churchill or Attlee had articulated would have fallen on deaf ears. If indeed it was Basildon Man and Woman who had won Thatcher her three terms, Major his, and Blair in turn his, who had time to listen to the disparate and isolated voices of the crofter, the gamekeeper, the tractor driver?

The stark reality for country people in twenty-first-century Britain is that they will never wield the stick that political arithmetic in France or America gives their counterparts in those countries. But does the anti-rural bias of national politics matter? And if so, what can be done to heal the town–country divide? The contributors to this book have emphatically answered yes to the first question. They offer a variety of answers to the second.

Simon Jenkins is a quintessentially metropolitan figure. It was his love and knowledge of London church architecture which led to a publisher's invitation to write his book on a thousand English parish churches. The surprise, anger, and dismay which have informed his analysis of contemporary rural Britain, set out here, with his special passion reserved for the depredations of prairie farming and the obliteration by housing of green fields, are all the more powerful given the background to his travels. Yet Matt Ridley and Mark Pennington argue that in the long term the preservation of landscape is best advanced by the deregulation of land use.

There is a major dilemma, as between enterprise and political action, to be resolved here.

We developed a decade ago the argument that Britain has the finest man-made landscape in the world. The concept of wilderness, as in North America, is alien to us, and perhaps the few pure wildernesses of Britain are at this point least vulnerable to the creeping threats of urbanisation. But for the first time ever in these islands' history we can identify the following dismal proposition. Unless there is a concerted social and political will on all sides to preserve and strengthen the rural community and the rural economy then we are in danger of losing for ever the commitment and experience which preserve the landscape, be it managed or wilderness.

THE WAY FORWARD

We are at a crucial moment in the evolution of these issues. On the one hand, there is a bitter and disenchanted mood abroad in rural Britain which in itself is both polarising and uniting rural opinion. We must at all costs avoid rural politics becoming sectarian. On the other, environmental issues are moving to centre stage in domestic politics in the developed world, most particularly here given the unique pressures of population on countryside. It is crucial that the dialogue be constructive and the outcome fruitful.

The Countryside Agency in its current survey of rural Britain, *The State of the Countryside 2000,* offered a bland and reassuring picture, skirting round most of the difficulties raised here while providing a useful and thorough statistical snapshot. But it did draw attention, under 'Public Perception of the Countryside', to the very real subliminal concern for the rural condition which the 1999 British Social Attitudes Survey flushed out:

- 90% believed the countryside provided a healthier environment to live in

- While only 18% lived in a rural location, nearly 50% said they would like to do so

- 84% expressed concern 'about things that may happen to the countryside'

- 75% considered the countryside should be protected from development, even at the cost of fewer jobs

- 80% agreed that 'it is more important to keep green-belt areas than to build new houses there'

- 73% agreed that 'new houses should be built in cities, towns, and villages rather than in the countryside'

- 88% considered that industry should be prevented from causing damage to the countryside even at the cost of higher prices

- Despite 69% criticising modern farming methods for causing damage, 77% felt that farmers do a good job in looking after the countryside.

Last autumn a *Daily Telegraph* Gallup poll said that over 80% feared the countryside was being destroyed by modern farming methods, pollution, the building of roads, houses and shopping malls. Over two-thirds would ban pesticides and herbicides, end new housing developments and ban malls.

All this suggests not only a much stronger level of support for the countryside and country people in our towns and cities than has been recognised, but also a deeper level of sympathy and understanding than country people would acknowledge. In short, Simon Jenkins is touching a strong chord in his lament for what he has seen.

However, enthusiasm for the countryside is matched by ignorance of it. Most respondents in the *Daily Telegraph* poll knew what a plough was for, but more than 40% could not correctly identify harvest time. Many thought that country people held harvest festivals in the spring. More than half said they had never seen a badger in the wild.

At the same time the Royal Agricultural Society of England (RASE) offered, in its powerfully argued *Routes to Rural Prosperity*, a bleak view of agriculture at the centre of the rural debate: 'The debate about the future of agriculture is of poor quality and lacking in vision. Through lack of clear policy we are on the brink of meltdown in farming. We need to find the balance where a thriving agriculture delivers a thriving rural landscape. It is time for completely new thinking for the British countryside and agriculture.'

As we go to press, the reputation of MAFF is hardly being enhanced as the foot-and-mouth crisis develops. Abigail Woods' disturbing piece suggests a serious failure to learn from the 1967 and 1981 outbreaks and thus have in readiness a fully-prepared game plan to deal with a new outbreak.

In the twenty years from 1971 to 1991 the membership of the National Trust rose from 278,000 to 2,152,000, that of the RSPB from 98,000 to 852,000. The charge against the leadership of both these organisations is that they behave in a manner which they believe will appeal to their urban members rather than taking responsibility for educating their new membership in the realities of rural life. But those numbers suggest a huge shift of urban interest and leisure activity.

Perhaps this gives hopeful ammunition to the proposition at the heart of this book. For if rural campaigning remains just that, a rural pressure group fighting for what it believes to be its own interests in a hostile environment, it will continue to exist only at the margin of mainstream politics.

The future for what rural Britain holds most dear, the preservation of the rural way of life, the strengthening and invigoration of the rural economy, the pride in and love for our inherited landscape, lies in reaching out to the huge metropolitan and urban majority and inviting it, through a better knowledge and understanding of the countryside which in every case surrounds our towns and cities, to claim ownership of and take responsibility for the rural issues. They will not, and should not, sign up to a pastoral idyll embedded in the past and sustained by parodies of rural life. The countryside as a theme park is total anathema to country people. And, as Nick Way points out in his essay, a realistic and thought-out programme of access to the countryside is now both expected and welcome. Our cities must be shown a tough-minded, proud, dynamic and realistic vision for a rural Britain with which they can identify.

A FOCUS FOR THE FUTURE

Threading through all the contributions to this book are three main issues: the erosion of landscape by pollution, over-intensification and planning disaster; the atrophy of the rural economy and way of life; the ever-widening gulf of misunderstanding between town and country. If these perceptions are correct, if it matters, and if we are to save the inheritance of our countryside for posterity, there is a simple and stark logic to be applied.

The unique characteristics of the British landscape will not survive without a thriving rural population. There must be a concerted strategy to keep people on the land by promoting the growth of the rural economy in the widest and most modern sense. There must be a new approach to planning whose top priorities are the preservation of landscape combined with an elasticity which allows local initiatives in rural business to develop and an approach to housing focused on meeting the needs of the indigenous rural population. There must be an imaginative and resourced strategy to attract city dwellers to visit and bond with the countryside and towards a deeper understanding of the richness as well as the problems of rural life.

I do not believe that any of these objectives are being pursued with commitment and clear thinking. They will not be pursued unless their importance to the health of the nation is accepted. The first token of this is to upgrade the importance of rural and environmental issues within government. The office of Secretary of State for the Countryside should become one of the great offices of state. It should be a spending department. It would, after all, be responsible for over 75% of the land mass of our country. And is it too much to hope that this post should always be held by someone who has a deep-rooted attachment to the countryside? An obvious way to follow the logic and pursue the objectives set out above would be that in this department there should be three portfolios: the first, Agriculture; the second, Landscape and Rural Environment, and the third combining responsibility for the rural economy, tourism and information. There is much talk now of rural proofing, i.e. considering all new legislation in terms of its impact on the countryside. If there were to be a comprehensive Department of the Countryside, by the same token urban proofing would apply, thus considering when rural initiatives and urban programmes, most particularly in terms of urban regeneration, overlap.

1 Agriculture

CAP is a fact of life. We await its reform, but farming policy is paralysed by this wait. We must think ahead and fashion a new way of farming which is built on the natural strengths of Britain. It is ridiculous that the arguments for organic farming which Professor Spedding espouses seem largely to be conducted in political rather than logical terms. In 1999 the Government spent £52 million on developing GM crops. It spent just £1.7 million on promoting organic farming. The proportion of our collective household budget spent on food decreases steadily. It must surely be the case that paying more for organic food, bought locally, will become an increasingly popular option. We must hope for a future in which the word 'subsidy' is no longer part of the rural vocabulary. Instead we should mean proper payment for support. Or at least we must make a very clear distinction between a pernicious and a virtuous subsidy! We want to see it replaced by the notion of realistic and enduring payment for the provision of goods and services, with the many and varied facets of preserving landscape and natural habitat very much part of services. John Gummer here makes a powerful case for switching CAP payments to the environment.

Production subsidies in particular have shielded farmers from market forces. We must achieve a policy where agriculture's role in land management and environmental care is combined with accepting the realities of the market. In pulling together the arguments advanced in this book in the section 'The Farm of the Future', we can't do better than quote the conclusions reached by the RASE in *Routes to Rural Prosperity*:

Food production will account for a smaller proportion of land use with farming adjusting to the provision of other goods. Farmers have to ask themselves: What does the market require? How much can I sell? How much can I produce?

Farmers remaining in food production will follow one of two routes:

- low-cost commodity production
- low-volume, high-value products filling niche markets, selling on distinctiveness.

Other farmers will develop their roles as land managers:

- producing energy and industrial crops
- diversifying out of agriculture into tourism, recreational or industrial services
- managing the land for environmental good, with this activity paid for in its own right.

Not all those currently engaged in farming have a long-term future in the industry. With the trend for agricultural incomes irreversibly in decline, all farmers need to think the unthinkable. For farmers to earn a decent living they need to be either fewer in number or pursuing a non-food farming income.

Agriculture will continue to be multifunctional. Food is only one of the possible outputs from land. Energy and environmental goods are essential, and legitimate outputs and new methods of finance and delivery are needed.

The status quo is not an option. The reality is that agricultural restructuring is inevitable and necessary. Farmers will be land managers and must grasp the opportunities for rural enterprise to create new markets for agricultural, environmental and landscape goods. Agriculture does have a prosperous future and is central to the vitality of rural communities.

In short, we must change from a programme of direct CAP subsidy of £3.5 billion a year to a future of integrated rural support.

2 Environment and Landscape

I believe personally, with Simon Jenkins, that it must be only a matter of time before there is a total ban on developing greenfield sites at least in the crowded areas of southern and central England. I accept that this would have considerable impact on house prices in those areas. But in those areas the real and growing scarcity is rural landscape. Rural building should surely focus exclusively on the needs of local housing. The Rural Housing Trust believes that close to 80,000 affordable homes are needed in rural England, and that a yield of £150 million a year from the abolition of the 50% discount on council tax given to owners of second homes would subsidise 5,700 of them every year. But this is political dynamite, and in this book Matt Ridley and Mark Pennington offer thoughtful appraisals of how planning regulations can be modernised to bring logic and purpose to the use of rural land in future. They are at one in advocating the de-nationalisation of the countryside, the removal of the plethora of controls that stultify and inhibit the initiatives which should legitimately flow from the ownership of land. There cannot, for example, be anyone involved in farming who is not appalled at the demise of rural abattoirs. We see the consequences of this when foot-and-mouth strikes. At the same time, as Graham Cox argues, there is an urgent and challenging need to think clearly about our obligations to the natural world. Not just the environment, but an attitude, a way of being, is under threat. Like Emerson and Thoreau in nineteenth-century America, we must have a doctrine and an agenda for self-improvement with restraint. We have an obligation to the land. It is possible to live wisely and respectfully on the land, and to live well. Roger Scruton makes the case that the landscape owes its fertility and beauty to the fact of private ownership, and that this must be made into an effective form of trusteeship, 'so that all of us can benefit from property which only some of us control'.

3 Rural Economy, Tourism and Information

In her essay, Dawn Goodfellow, Director of the Countryside Foundation for Education, points out that current lifestyles have divorced the majority of the population from any connection with the natural world. But she believes that we can succeed in educating people about the reality and significance of the countryside. There must be a whole-hearted commitment to achieve this.

Aside from the prescriptions for a healthy future for farming which we have discussed, hand-in-glove with diverse initiatives for the rural economy must be a programme of information and long-term education to bridge the gap to which our contributors continually return, a refrain which echoes throughout this book.

The face of rural Italy has been transformed in recent years by the government programme of *Agritourism*, the manifesto for which is attached here as an appendix. It is publicly funded, and it has been a huge success. It has encouraged communities and individuals in every part of Italy to develop every facet of tourism and information – facilities, historic attractions, paths and byways, accommodation, and not least food. Spain has recently and successfully followed this example. I believe that a public- and private-sector partnership in Britain, very much involving the new Ministry as co-ordinator and even part-financier, offering tremendous opportunities for sponsorship at a national and local level, would not only be hugely successful but could also result in a uniquely comprehensive, attractive and informative road map of rural Britain.

Side by side with this should go a whole-hearted commitment to promoting all manifestations of a thriving modern rural economy to take its place beside the new realities of agriculture.

There is no one magic solution to any of this. The essence of the problem is its diversity. But there is a challenging ministerial portfolio in prospect to bring this together and to imprint success on the face of the British countryside. It should include an opportunity for an imaginative national directory of the countryside, incorporating all tourist facilities. Hand in glove with this goes the obvious need for affordable Internet access. The current Countryside and Rights of Way Act will surely not survive in its present form, and the next Parliament will bring a renewed opportunity to apply logic to the whole question of off-road access in the constructive spirit offered by Nick Way here. There are myriad opportunities for the revitalisation of farmers' markets and market towns, as in the Yorkshire and Humber scheme, to integrate with new patterns of local production. And surely, in these desperately difficult times, there is a justifiable resonance about Buy British which goes beyond the chauvinistic.

There should be a national scheme of sponsored awards for the upkeep and promotion of local facilities, bridleways, cycleways and rights of way – all designed so that the whole range of rural attractions and facilities catches the imagination of our towns and cities.

Above all, country and town are inextricably bound in a common predicament. It may be that only urban regeneration, and above all the imaginative development of brownfield sites, will eventually save the landscape. Can changes in urban policy diminish the legitimate urge to escape the blighted townscapes?

If we can move forward on these fronts, and if we can forge broader alliances, then surely our despairing question, 'Does it matter?' begins to answer itself.

APPENDIX: AGRITOURISM

Translated from an Italian Government Briefing

AGRITOURISM
Set up in Rome 12/2/65

1. Objectives
If you join Agritourism you take part in . . .

- The development of a tourism in the country which respects agriculture, the natural environment and the many cultural differences which there are in the world of the countryside.
- A confirmation of a new cultural enterprise in agriculture which prizes the quality of the product, a conscience about ecology, the role of soil protection and the prevention of hydrological failures.
- The defence of typical food production methods of our agriculture, the appreciation of regional wine production and the construction of a fully developed food culture.
- The maintenance of the countryside with its old buildings, traditional farming methods and the flora of the Mediterranean countryside.
- The establishment of a fertile and well-balanced cultural exchange between town and countryside to establish a better quality of life for everyone.

2. The members
Agritourism is an association which is open to everyone:

- The ordinary members include farm owners of every sort, whether they participate or not in *agriturismo* or in general country tourism but who wish to help achieve something for their enterprise.
- The *adherent* members, in the various forms as set out by the statute, are all the others (individuals, public or private companies) who are passionate about 'farm holidays' or aware of the environmental and cultural tourist problems and who intend to achieve something for their enterprise.
- The ordinary members come under the provincial Sections or Regional Associations of Agritourism (i.e. *province e regioni*) which give assistance on specific matters concerning the management of the enterprise. The *adherent* members come under the national Association of Agritourism which offers them information and tourism services.

3. Activities

- Agritourism achieves its social aims through activities and services addressed to public institutions and members.

Public institutions
- From European to national, regional or local, it carries out a constant stream of proposals and courses of action in order that the development policy is in line with the aims of the enterprise.

Farm and technical business people (ordinary members)
- It carries out constant trade union activities to look after the interests of the various categories with particular reference to new laws and regulations that favour the development of the projects along the lines of the enterprise's aims.

- It offers an opportunity for the exchange of experiences and the solution of business problems which are of general interest.
- It offers an information service on business management (organisation, legislation, administration), promotes accommodation possibilities to the general public (guides, link-ups with computer networks, demonstrations) and carries out business training courses.

For tourists (adherent members)
- It sets out full information on farm holidays, rural itineraries, purchase of typical food products, areas of environmental protection.
- It organises services which facilitate holiday organisation by booking places to stay and offering special deals on them.
- It carries out a constant control on the quality offered by the farms.
- It keeps up to date on matters that relate to the company activity, and asks for opinions about the best ways to help.

For all the members
- It draws up a reference point in order to maintain initiatives and especially to promote and establish
  - development of the countryside which respects the natural resources
  - careful land management which is based on its protection
  - complete safeguard of environmental resources
  - care of the traditional ways of the countryside
  - defence of typical food production
  - preservation of historical tales about rural life
  - a balanced exchange of culture between town and country
  - dissemination of information about agriculture and its products in schools

1. Publications
Agritourism members, according to their category, can receive free:

Guide to Rural Accommodation, which gives details of all agritourism establishments and all that they offer.

Agritourism Magazine three-monthly, which offers tours etc. and gives information (some previously unpublished).

As well as these two magazines Agritourism produces regional guides, thematic guides such as *Guide to Farm Products* and technical brochures for operators and socio-economic studies.

2. Offices

Agritourism is a national organisation broken down into regional and provincial organisations. The head office handles all the tourist and general information and the other offices take care of assistance to the farms.

NOTES ON CONTRIBUTORS

Michael Sissons was until recently Chairman of the Peters Fraser & Dunlop Group and was a founder of the Countryside Movement.

Professor Lord Skidelsky is the author of the highly acclaimed three-volume biography of Keynes and Chairman of the Social Market Foundation

Professor Roger Scruton was Professor of Philosophy at Birkbeck College and is the author of sixteen books, including *Animal Rights and Wrongs* and *On Hunting*.

Simon Jenkins writes regular columns for *The Times* and the *Evening Standard*. He has edited both newspapers. His latest book is *England's Thousand Best Churches*.

Hon. Dr Matt Ridley is the author of *Genome*, *The Origins of Virtue*, and other books on science. He writes a regular column for the *Daily Telegraph*.

Dr Mark Pennington is a lecturer in Public Policy at Queen Mary College. He has written widely on the political economy of planning and environmental policy, including his book *Planning and the Political Market*.

Alan Kilkenny OBE is an independent public-relations consultant with professional interests in rural affairs and a close attachment to the countryside.

Rt Hon. John Gummer MP was Minister of Agriculture, Fisheries and Food from 1989 to 1993 and Secretary of State for the Environment from 1993 to 1997.

Caroline Hitchman has a Masters Degree in Public Health and Nutrition from the London School of Hygiene and Tropical Medicine. She has conducted a study of poverty in the Forest of Dean for Demos.

Professor Sir Colin Spedding is Emeritus Professor at the

University of Reading. He chaired the UK Register of Organic Food Standards until 1999, and the Farm Animal Welfare Council from 1988 to 1998.

Graham Harvey has been story editor of *The Archers* and is the author of *The Killing of the Countryside*.

Hugh Oliver-Bellasis farms in Hampshire. He chaired the Food Standards Committee of the National Farmers' Union and represented Hampshire on its Council until 1999. He was awarded a Fellowship of the Royal Agricultural Societies in 1992.

Abigail Woods is a PhD student in the History of Foot-and-Mouth Disease in Twentieth-Century Britain at the Wellcome Unit for the History of Medicine, Manchester University. Her article represents work in progress.

Graham Cox is Senior Lecturer in the Faculty of Humanities and Social Sciences at the University of Bath and has researched and published extensively on agriculture, the politics of the countryside, and environmental change.

Nick Way is Chief Political Adviser to the Country Land and Business Association.

Dawn Goodfellow is Chief Executive of the Countryside Foundation for Education.